T0272660

Expressive Printmaking

a creative guide

Mary Dalton

Expressive Printmaking

a creative guide

❊ THE CROWOOD PRESS

First published in 2022 by
The Crowood Press Ltd
Ramsbury, Marlborough
Wiltshire SN8 2HR

enquiries@crowood.com
www.crowood.com

This impression 2024

© Mary Dalton 2022

All rights reserved. No part of this publication may be reproduced or transmitted in any
form or by any means, electronic or mechanical, including photocopy, recording, or
any information storage and retrieval system, without permission in writing from the
publishers.

British Library Cataloguing-in-Publication Data
A catalogue record for this book is available from the British Library.

ISBN 978 0 7198 4103 3

Cover design: Sergey Tsvetkov

Typeset by Chennai Publishing Services
Printed and bound in India by Nutech Print Services - India

CONTENTS

	Introduction	6
1	Getting Started with Ink	9
2	Relief Work: Vegetable Stamping and Beyond	21
3	Spontaneous Monochromes in a Single Pull	43
4	Expressive Paper Dry-Point	65
5	Mokulito	89
6	Lithino	115
7	Collage in Printmaking	133
8	Inks and Colour Effects	149
9	Celebrating the Unique: Print Beyond Paper	167
10	Workshop Basics	187
	Stockists and Resources	205
	Index	206

INTRODUCTION

What do you think about when I say 'print-making'? Perhaps some old lino that was reluctantly carved into many years ago? Perhaps this old lino was actually cracking and smelt slightly odd? Perhaps you think of screen-printed t-shirt designs or lots of small businesses hand printing greetings cards? Most likely there will be some notion of being able to create more than one of the same image, what we refer to as an edition.

Printmaking has many images and stereotypes amongst the general population who are interested in the arts. It sits on a very perilous fence between drawing and applied art, painting and craft, digital and handmade, reproduction and unique. It seems not to have its own category, something that may seem at first confusing, but actually it means it can be anything you want it to be. And isn't that glorious? This book will take you on a journey through the more dynamic approaches to learning the techniques of printmaking so that it can be moulded into your own language. We will look briefly at editioning, but it will not be the focus or the main event because *art is unique*. This includes printmaking. It has so much potential that I only begin to explore in the following chapters, so many ways of communicating feeling; the textures and forms of the printed impression sing so loudly that words and editions are not needed.

Treat this book as your guide: a way to explore these unique and dynamic ways of working whilst being given permission to let loose. Whilst you have a supportive ear, you can try out new approaches with energy and vigour knowing questions will be listened to and answered. This book leads you down a path towards understanding printmaking as an art form unlike any other and as unique as them all. Once that path is walked, it will be such fun and so energizing, that you may not turn back.

The chapters build in momentum and can be read sequentially, developing your technique and confidence, or they can be dipped into individually. Even if you are an experienced printmaker, why not try some of the exercises that may seem aimed towards beginners? Who knows, by trying an approach outside of your daily practice, it may trigger something unexpected. It is always good to re-learn skills from a different educational angle.

But of course, what is most important is to have fun. Fun and play are crucial to learning, skills that as adults we so easily relegate to our childhood years. Well, now is the time to bring it back and embrace it. Through playing we actually learn far more and learn it with more studiousness because we are freely engaging with it. We are able to be more direct with our feelings and our communication and the resulting print is awesomely stronger. Printmaking for all! Printmaking for fun!

HOW THIS BOOK WORKS

This book is a process-led book, placing the emphasis upon guiding the reader how to build confidently in printed expression, rather than purely feeding technical facts to you. There are numerous follow-along projects that are guided but also loose enough to allow you to take your own spin on the inspiration and thus the outcome. The projects are useful to aid the understanding of practical elements of the printed medium as well as how these technical elements may influence expression.

The book covers relief, planographic and intaglio methods of printmaking. The planographic areas include monoprint and the lithographic chapters. Each chapter has its own specific topic to cover, but as the chapters develop, they will freely reference and take influence from techniques already covered throughout the book. The chapters can sit alone, but they are best assimilated in conjunction with a brief understanding of preceding topics. It is vital to understand that the emphasis of this book is on producing unique prints. They are rarely designed to be editioned. Thus, when chapters freely take influence from each other, it leads to building very complex and expressive works.

I hope you enjoy reading this book. More than this, I hope you get inky fingers on its corners, flick through the pages with joy, excitement, trepidation and absolute wonder at what the possibilities are for making art. Expression is a vital part of being human. Open eyes, minds and hearts and look – really look – at what stories you wish to tell through the glorious medium of printmaking, and I can promise you, print will tell those stories with a firm punch of what it is to be human.

ENVIRONMENTAL STANDARDS

The planet and its environment need all the support we can give. Printmaking, as with many commercial industries, is at odds with improving environmental standards. Many of the commercial printmaking processes are not healthy for the planet, but the industry is taking small steps towards improvement. Artist printmakers have a greater ability to shape their own practice to aid the planet and their own health. We can choose what we use in our studios and how we take care of the waste that leaves. It truly is important that as individuals we begin to make changes in day-to-day studio practice to help the future of this planet. It is not impossible either. Small changes in operations do not need to mean grand shifts in practice, they just incrementally make a change for the better. Furthermore, these small achievable targets start to educate those around us that it is possible.

This book, where at all possible, adheres to quite tight environmental practice. Toxic clean-up chemicals are not used, rainwater is used where possible to replace tap water, items are encouraged to be re-used and recycled, non-toxic oil-based ink is used throughout, and the processes that we learn about are, for the most part, leaving a pretty clean footprint behind us.

Printmaking ink is a vital part of the artist's practice and one that is open to huge debate. Many options are available on the market, and it can often be confusing. The reasons I advocate traditional oil-based ink throughout this book are long and well researched. My personal choice is taken through reading many Material Safety Data Sheets (MSDS), looking at studies and generally making a considered decision within the facts I am able to obtain. For this reason I use traditional oil-based printing inks, made with non-toxic pigments and with no added modifiers or driers.

The end decision with all these small steps rests with yourself. I will offer tips and hints on how to change personal practice to be cleaner and have less of an impact upon the planet, but you have to make the change. The planet is suffering, that is a fact, and we need to help it. In Chapter 10 (Workshop Basics), we will look at day to day changes and operational decisions that can help you express with a lighter footprint. Key to all of this is to take time out and research the processes and materials with the facts you can obtain through MSDS and research papers. It does not take long, but I feel it is vital if we are to change the way printmaking operates and the impact it has upon the planet.

CHAPTER 1

GETTING STARTED WITH INK

To understand printmaking and its full expressive potential we need to look at what print is. This is not a historical analysis nor a technical breakdown of the printmaking family tree; instead we need to creatively explore the essence of what differentiates a print from other forms of visual expression. In this chapter we will take it back to the beginning and look at how we can create unique, bold, dynamic prints from the most limited supplies. In some ways, the processes in the chapter may seem simplistic, but the emphasis here is on resetting a way of thinking about print, not just a way of doing. Through an exploration of the essence of printmaking and by taking things back to the start, new doors often open to rekindle expression. This chapter will start a journey on changing the way we think about print and how we may explore printmaking without any judgement upon technique, aesthetic, or facilities. Let's start over.

WHAT IS PRINTMAKING?

There is huge debate amongst artists as to what a print is, especially with the advent of digital technologies and their influence upon printmaking. I fall into the category of printmaking by hand. This means there is a print plate, which I refer to as the matrix, which receives ink, which then gets transferred onto a substrate (e.g. paper) to produce an impression. Thus we have a matrix, some ink and an impression. This is how I see printmaking and, yes, it may seem incredibly understated for what printmaking can offer, but it highlights the process by which print differs from other mediums. A hand print or a finger print is simple, but it is print.

Artists often refer to printmaking to describe an image that can be editioned. This has categorically nothing to do with

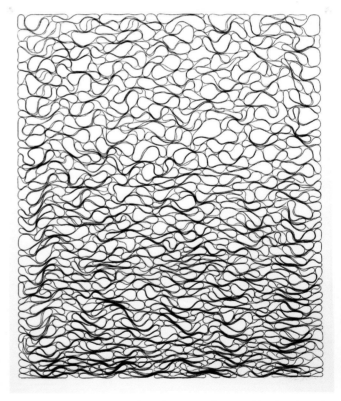

Untitled, 2006, Tara Donovan, ink on Kozo paper from a rubber band matrix, 52″ × 42″ (132.1cm × 106.7cm). (Photo: Kerry Ryan McFate, courtesy Pace Gallery © Tara Donovan)

the essence of printmaking and what it can offer the artist. A print does not need to be editioned to be a print. In fact, the majority of techniques and works we explore in this book are not editioned, instead they explore the expressive qualities of unique printmaking. Editioning has huge value and place within print, and of course is an element of the art form that does not exist in a similar fashion in other media, such as painting. However, it is a business, artistic and personal choice to edition; it does not define printmaking.

Do We Really Need all that Equipment?

No, you do not. Printmaking is notorious for needing a huge amount of specialist equipment that can not only cost a huge amount of money but can also become a way to distract the artist from actually making something. Printmaking studios are full of lovely rollers lined up, little tools in boxes, tins of strange liquids and potions, pencils, needles, baths, tanks, papers, glues, inks, presses, hot-plates, more rollers, metal, plastic, card, scrapers, roulettes.... On top of this the techniques of printmaking are so vast and huge and gloriously endless, that it can all be overwhelming for both the beginner and the more experienced artist. Many people new to printmaking are daunted with so much information, that they are quivering before they even get a chance to put ink onto paper. It is so important to not let the material requirements for the technical elements of printmaking prevent you from freely expressing. So, let's move on from all those materials and tools at the very beginning and approach them as and when needed. We will be starting out from the most fundamental of materials that allow us to generate a matrix, apply ink, and create an impression on paper. The items for printmaking in this chapter should all be readily available. Let's form a new way to approach printmaking, a new way to think about printmaking. This is Chapter 1, where we shall be starting from the essence of print and taking it on a wonderful journey to its explosion in Chapter 9, witnessing where dynamic printmaking can really go.

Printmaking is unpredictable, feisty, fun, glorious, and most of all it is uniquely expressive. It is an awesome medium that can bring joy to all, old and young.

Ink

Throughout this book, the projects and demonstrations are created using traditional printmakers' oil-based ink, which is linseed oil and a pigment ground together. There are water washable oil-based inks on the market nowadays; however, their properties are different from traditional oil-based inks which I refer to. There are three main reasons for the use of oil-based inks in this book. Firstly, they have a very slow drying time, thus allowing you to have all your ink out all day and you never need have to worry about constantly cleaning it up or it drying on your equipment. This means you can have a full experiment and play without having to stop, vital for many of the projects in this book. Secondly, certain techniques that we cover will

We will be focusing on using oil-based ink throughout this book.

Linseed oil is the main binder used in traditional printing inks.

Traditional oil-based relief printing ink in deep pink being ground by Cranfield Colours. Traditional inks of such high quality and colour strength such as these are beautiful to work with.

only work with oil-based inks, such as lithography. Thirdly, the environmental debate regarding inks, as discussed in the environmental section, has strengthened my reasoning for using traditional oil-based ink. Do not be put off by cleaning oil-based inks at home. They do clean up with standard vegetable oil and a cotton rag – no solvents needed.

So how is oil-based printmaking ink made? And why is it different to oil paint? Oil-based ink, like oil paint, consists of ground pigment and oil (traditionally linseed oil). Linseed oil is described as a 'drying' oil. Oils fall into two categories, drying oils and non-drying oils. You need inks to be ground with drying oils, otherwise you would have a very oily, wet print for a very, very long time. Olive oil is a non-drying oil. Sunflower oil is a partially drying oil, with a slower drying time than linseed. It is naturally yellow, and so not a great binder when really making high-quality inks. Linseed oil dries fully and can be heated and reduced down to produce different viscosities of oil. When the linseed oil is heat treated, in printmaking it is generally referred to as plate oil or copper plate oil. It comes in various viscosities to adjust the ink's consistency.

Printing ink is much tackier than oil paint, allowing it to stay in the incised lines of intaglio or sit evenly on relief matrix and not slip around. But in both instances, pigment is ground with the oil until the two materials are bonded together and the ink is a smooth consistency, with no gritty particles of pigment. Ink manufacturers have a multitude of wondrous recipes for ratios of different oil, pigments and grinds, all of which work in unison to produce a high-quality printing ink. For the purposes of this book, we will be using a pre-made traditional printmaking ink. However, making your own printing ink is a wonderful exploration of materials science and is well worth the journey if and when you choose.

PROJECT

MAKING A PRINT

In this guided project we will be looking at how to make a printing dolly and use it to help print an impression. The image we produce is not intended to be the most technically challenging print, but it is the result of an extraordinary journey that enables you to see what makes a print different to other means of artistic expression, both visually and technically. It is intended to allow you to get to know your materials and to see what can be done with the bare minimum.

Materials

- Oil-based black printing ink
- Paper of any description or size
- A selection of textured objects and surfaces
- A stable and non-absorbent solid surface approximately A4 that will get inky (e.g. piece of plastic or thick glass)
- A large, round smooth stone that fits in your hand
- Two pieces of old cotton (e.g. pillowcase) approximately 30cm square
- String

Workspace

Any space you can find. You will not be using a press. You will need the non-absorbent sheet to be very stable, so if you have a wobbly table, work on the floor if you are able. The non-absorbent sheet will be getting inky so please make appropriate precautions to its surroundings. You will also need a clean working area where you will be printing.

Printmaking Dolly

Printmakers' dollies were a traditional way to apply ink before the mass use of a printmaking roller. They are held in the hand and their soft, round 'head' is used to apply ink to the surface of the printing matrix. Traditionally made with leather and wood, and rather beautiful, we are going to emulate the principle with materials that you are more likely to have around. This homemade dolly may not last the rigours of decades in a print shop, but it will last this chapter (if not, it is easily repairable). The dolly made here is mainly for the purpose of this chapter for you to see what you can do from nothing, but you can use it for the other projects in this book, even if we switch to a roller. Once the dolly is made, we go on to use it to apply ink.

The Matrix

The matrix, as we briefly mentioned, is the element of printmaking that receives the ink, for instance a linocut, an etching plate, a lithographic stone. In this very first chapter, we will be using textured items from around the home as our matrices. This could be a bit of lace, an orange peel, corrugated card, scrunched foil, a plastic dinosaur foot – basically, anything that has a flat surface element to it that we may apply ink to and create a stamp.

The impression we will be building will take inspiration from a singular object from around you. The choice of object is important, as it needs to be something that means something to you and that you want to express. Emotion plays a huge role in expression, so let's engage with it now. The object will also need a few textures upon it so that we have something to get to

The sample materials required to make the printmaking dolly.

Lay the fabric strips in the middle with the stone on the top.

Gather all four corners to the top and hold tightly together.

Use the yarn to bind around the fabric, creating a handle.

The finished basic dolly will serve you well in this chapter.

A vast array of materials will produce interesting printed marks.

Cut out the silhouette of the object free-form with scissors.

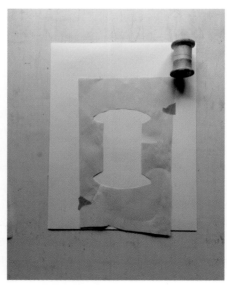

Loosely tape the mask down in place on your printing paper.

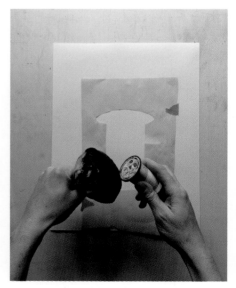

Apply ink to the preferred object using your printing dolly.

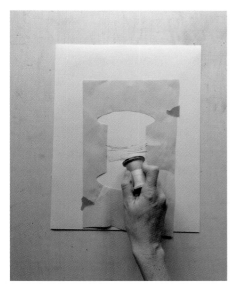

Use the object to create texture and marks within the mask.

You can use the dolly itself to generate areas of darkness.

Tools unrelated to your object may print interesting marks.

Continue to build up textural information within the print.

When complete, very gently peel away the tape and the mask.

The completed print will have both strong texture and form.

grips with. This project will also introduce the principles of mask making, that is, using paper to protect areas of the paper whilst you print upon others. Masks are used throughout the book and it is important we see their value early on.

Have fun using the dolly to apply ink to your textured surfaces and representing the object you have chosen. If need be, test a texture on a scrap of paper before you print on your actual impression. Many questions arise when printing with these techniques: Is there a preferred amount of ink to get a clean image? Can you create multiple prints from the same material? What happens if you do not reapply ink before stamping? If there are any particular results you enjoy, note them down as they may have an input later on.

LOOKING AT THE TOOLS UPSIDE DOWN

Shapes and patterns and textures exist all around us all of the time. Sometimes it is difficult to see how a cork stamp can look like nothing more than a mottled moon. Or a piece of lace, well, like a piece of lace. Understanding the essence of printmaking, from the ink to the matrix to the substrate, needs to be explored freely alongside how we see things in relationship to print. Printmaking has a huge amount of making in its process, and thus a huge amount of mark-making, from scratching with needles to stamping with corks. However, it is difficult in an art form so full of information and controls to see beyond the cork stamp being more than just the image of a moon. Here we take a look at a few materials in more detail to see how a different approach to their use can completely change the mark.

Cork

If you use a basic cork to make a few stamps, it is how we expected: a mottled round shape resembling some moon face. What if we are to roll the cork on its side edge and repeat this action with energetic motions? The marks are quite beautiful and extraordinarily different from moon face. If you integrate this rolling technique with a mask you can generate some very dynamic forms. Still printing, just with a simple, fun twist.

Corrugated Cardboard

Corrugated cardboard comes in so many different forms and patterns. Have a rummage around and see what you can find. If you are able to peel away the top layer to reveal the corrugation

A humble cork can produce varying effects if explored fully.

Using a paper mask adds a bold and crisp edge to the marks.

The mask allows a definite textural shape to be generated.

There are many types of corrugated card with varying textures.

Try building a cross hatch, peeling or printing on its side.

A range of marks can be explored, from edges to surface area.

strips underneath, these print beautifully. It is a hugely versatile print medium for textural effects and can be layered very successfully to create tonal value. Do not forget to use the edges of the card, as some of them have wonderful zig-zags running along the cut edge. Have a play with texture and also a basic mask, as with the cork.

Netting

Netting is so versatile and can be used with many different approaches. The tonal work created through the inked netting is created through the build-up of layers. The build-up of a netting stamp, with all its cross hatches, highlights how a printed impression is built up of these layers, each one independent in application but integrating with each other in the end result. It is a very unusual way of thinking and one that may take some time to get used to, but that is not uncommon. It is fun, complex, and exciting, and very much key to printmaking.

TOOLKIT OF MARKS

It can be very useful to make a series of tester sheets made from the marks of various objects to help guide your selection for your impression. This toolkit of textures can be quite extensive. Cut a selection of paper and on each sheet, print the first impression of the texture and the ghost. The first impression is when you ink

and stamp the object, producing a dark impression. The ghost is any subsequent stamping done without applying more ink to the object. It will inevitably produce a fainter impression, but also one that will be significantly different from the first impression.

Kettle, by Mary Dalton. A cast-iron kettle hand stamped through a mask using only netting from a bag of pony carrots. The varying use of the material has built up a sense of depth.

Print the first impression and the ghost on each sheet.

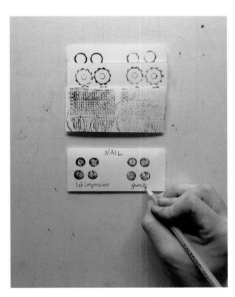

Each sample can be labelled and be used for reference.

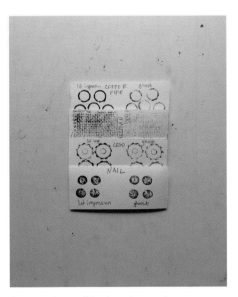

An extensive toolkit of varying mark-making tools.

CARDBOARD ROOM 'SKETCH'

This project will showcase exactly what can be done with just one material and a bit of imagination and play. You will be taking inspiration from the room view you see around you, so make sure you are in a setting in which you can refer to a suitable space.

Materials

- Corrugated card of varying textures and sizes, clean and free of detritus (tape can be left on)
- Ink
- Printmaking dolly
- Paper, smooth surface, white or off white, approximately A3 in size
- Inking area
- Scissors
- Craft knife
- Pile of clean tissue paper or newsprint, about ten A5 pieces
- Vegetable oil for clean-up
- Cotton rag

Image Making

To start with, you will need to assess your cardboard selection. Some corrugated card has a top layer that can easily peel away, revealing the lovely ridges underneath. Other varieties tear less well but instead have a beautiful edge section. Explore the card you have and find out its individual properties before delving into the ink. Play with tearing, cutting, and peeling the top surface, scrunching or stabbing the card, cutting it to shape with scissors or knife. After exploring the possibilities of the card, look around you and select a view that you feel you could have a fun go at representing. We will not be able to print tiny details like door knobs or individual leaves, but we

A varied selection of corrugated cardboard is vital.

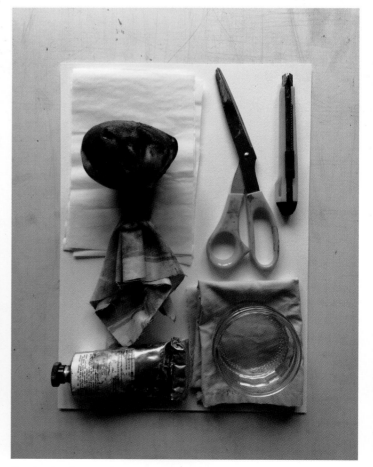

The simple selection of materials required for the project.

Embrace strong shapes and bold decisions to guide the print.

Note the type of the card and ink up to enhance the texture.

Use masks to protect any areas of the paper before printing.

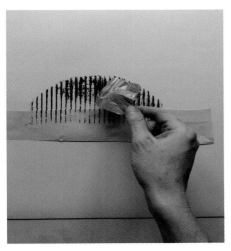

Card with tape on is fun to print, especially if scrunched.

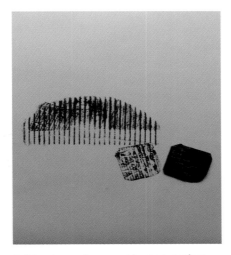

Build up layers, forms, and fun textures for a dynamic print.

Masks can protect printed areas when adding further layers.

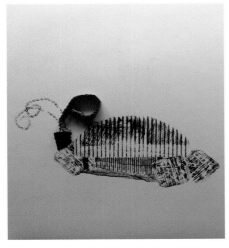

Using card on its side allows for a beautiful organic approach.

Details are useful in large empty spaces to keep interest.

The completed room 'sketch' printed in corrugated cardboard.

can have a good go at the impression of the space, the dynamics of its architecture and light. Once you have found a good space, set up your workspace and start printing. Think of how you can create a sense of depth using the card by applying more or less ink, pressing with a firmer or lighter pressure, or even building tone by using the corrugated stripes like cross hatching. Be bold with decisions and be bold with leaving some areas with no marks on at all. Prints need space to breathe. To keep your image clean, after you have placed the object in contact with the paper, before applying pressure, lay a piece of clean tissue paper or newsprint over it. This will prevent any inky fingers transferring fingerprints to your impression paper.

FINISHING UP

The techniques covered in this first chapter, and the basic principles of printmaking, will be developed throughout the book. This very first introduction, or even re-introduction for experienced printmakers, is about opening up to new possibilities and thinking about what print is, how it can be used as unique expression, and how we can engage with it playfully. As mentioned at the start of the chapter, we are retraining our minds as much as our technique.

The printmaking dolly can be used in most of the chapters of this book, although feel free to use a roller as well. The dolly is an example of making a print applicator at home and with little expenditure, but we will also be specifically using it for certain techniques later on.

Cleaning

Cleaning up oil-based ink is very easy. If you are using oil-based ink throughout, then the clean-up process is exactly the same after each project. Using a piece of firm card, a palette knife, or even an old plastic loyalty card, scrape up any spare ink. Place this into a scrap of paper and fold up to be binned. Large volumes of ink can be put onto some thick card and covered with a piece of foil to re-use another day. Once spare ink is removed, add about a 50p blob of oil to the centre of the inking area and spread around with the dolly. Cover all equipment with a film of oil and leave it for a couple of minutes. Using a clean cotton rag, wipe away the ink on the surface and on the dolly. Once surfaces are clean, and the dolly is wiped as best you can to take it back to a smooth, even surface, wipe fully over with a completely clean rag. The ink will never be completely removed from the dolly; instead, the oil-based ink will dry on the surface of the dolly in a small film, helping seal the cotton ready for next use.

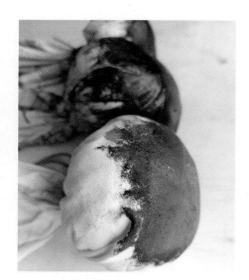
Home-made dollies will be used in this book for certain techniques.

Scrape up excess ink and place in scrap paper to be binned.

Using the rag, wipe a small amount of oil over the ink area.

Continue wiping with clean sections of the rag until clear.

Scrape off excess ink from the surface of the dolly and bin.

Using a small amount of oil, wipe the dolly top until smooth.

Use a mild soap solution and cloth to remove any residual oil.

CHAPTER 2

RELIEF WORK: VEGETABLE STAMPING AND BEYOND

Methods of relief printing have become hugely popular amongst artists as a way of an introduction to print. They require minimal set up and can be hand-printed, both of which are fantastic. The key factor with relief work is to prevent it becoming too repetitive, with similar imagery and motifs being used because they are graphically satisfying or easy to cut and print. Relief work can be dynamic and full of raw intuitive energy if we allow the tools to flow freely and the imagination take hold with alternative methods. Most objects around you produce a texture or pattern which can be combined with other methods of traditional relief work. This chapter will introduce a few of these approaches to alternative relief printmaking, which will hold you in great imaginative stead for creating energetic and unusual prints.

WHAT IS RELIEF PRINTING?

Relief printmaking describes a print created when ink sits on a raised surface of a matrix and an impression is taken from this. Linocut is a form of relief printing because the ink sits on the raised area of lino that is left after other areas have been carved away. Wood cut, wood engraving, potato stamping, cork carving, and plaster cast carving are all other methods of relief printmaking. Linocut is hugely powerful and versatile in its application for printmaking, particularly if you combine it with other methods. We will be exploring lino broadly as a means to create certain marks and effects, but we will also be looking at methods to create relief texture and prints with varying tools and materials that can be readily found around you. Relief printing is a very broad topic, so we are looking at the specific areas that are

The surface texture of different inks on a hand-printed impression is unique to relief work.

relevant to our end goal of creating dynamic prints with alternative methods. If you wish to further explore relief printmaking, this chapter should help keep your imagination open and your technique clean.

Linocut

Linocut is a great introduction to the principles of relief printing. Traditional artists' lino derives from linoleum flooring and is made with a mixture of linseed oil, bark and resin which is backed onto jute. Traditional lino is inert to humans and the environment and a great product for those who wish to pursue a more sustainable approach to their printmaking. It has a shelf life, and the natural ingredients will eventually go rancid after a few years; old lino can crack and be hard to carve. Fresh lino with sharp tools should be like cutting through hard butter. There are also alternatives to traditional lino on the market, made from vinyl or rubber. These can commonly be referred to as soft-cut or Japanese vinyl. These cut differently and are not biodegradable. But they sometimes offer less resistance and more ease of cutting for those with wrist, arm or shoulder difficulties. When using lino in this chapter, I will be using the traditional grey artists' lino. Traditional lino can also come in a dark brown or pale buff colour. All three varieties have slight nuances when it comes to the cutting, but the primary principles are exactly the same. I will be covering the basics of linocut as a means to an end to give you enough information to use it in conjunction with other relief methods. If lino is your calling, then please be assured there are many wonderful resources dedicated to its craft to help guide you.

Lino Tools, Traditional and Otherwise

Traditional linocut tools come in so many varieties and shapes that it is worth researching to find the ones you like. My advice tends to be to use a mid-range set to have a play, and then if you wish to pursue further you can invest in some higher-quality tools. I have six high-quality Swiss tools in my set that have served me well for over ten years. I require no more for my purposes. If, however, you have no lino tools with you now (and why would you necessarily?) then do not panic. Lino can be marked with numerous other household objects. Anything that will remove that top surface of lino and thus create a raised surface to receive ink, will generate an impression; for instance, a cheese grater, citrus zester, old dental tools, sandpaper and many more.

Surface Relief Printing

We have covered this briefly in the previous chapter, in which we applied ink to textures and took a basic impression. This is the absolute essence of the relief print; in this chapter we will develop this into a sophisticated and quality method of print-making. This may involve direct stamping or it may involve making an actual matrix. We have a whole array of techniques up our sleeves that can bring relief printing into a new dimension. As with the printing in Chapter 1, we will be treating much of the relief methods as unique prints. This is something that we follow throughout the book.

Unique prints, especially when it comes to relief printing, seem almost a contradiction in terms. To spend so much time

Traditional artists' lino is seductive and wonderful to cut into.

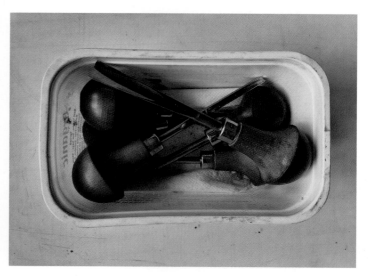

My personal and well-loved traditional linocut tools.

Unique relief prints are compelling, dynamic and challenge the artist in all directions.

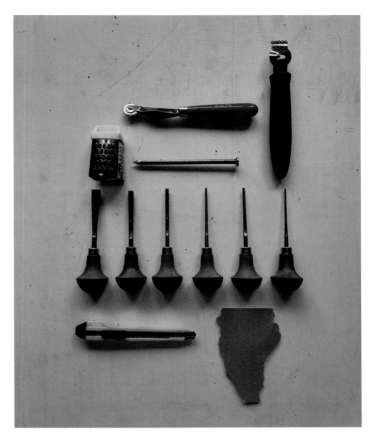

A range of tools suitable for carving traditional lino.

carving a linocut and to only use it once can indeed be confusing if one is trained in editioning or print as a means to replicate. This is why we must begin to unlearn and to sing relief print from the highest of mountains as a unique, sumptuous impression.

Materials

For the projects in the following chapter, you will need:

- Lino
  Traditional jute-backed lino will be used in the following chapters. This comes in grey or brown. You can replace with soft cut or Japanese vinyl if you so wish. You will need approximately two A4 pieces for the projects.
- Lino cutting tools
  A small set of traditional lino cutting tools is ideally needed, alongside a range of other tools from around the home that can make a mark in lino, such as a citrus zester, a grater, a nail. A craft knife, cutting mat and strong pair of scissors is required to cut lino.

- Ink
  We will be using oil-based relief ink. If you wish to use water-soluble relief ink, please check the manufacturer's guidelines on cleaning up and be careful not to get water on the back of the traditional lino, as it can cause it to buckle. We will be starting in monochrome, but we will also be using coloured ink. You will only need a 50p size amount of four or five different colours, which of course you can also mix together.
- Roller or dolly
  You can use your printing dolly for the monochrome print projects and if you wish to use a dolly for the colour work, you will need a separate dolly for each colour. This may seem time consuming, but you will inevitably use them again. A printmaking roller can also be used for all these projects; you will need to clean the roller before you switch to a new colour, or have separate rollers.
- Palette knives or old credit cards
  These are useful for ink mixing.
- Printing barren
  This helps apply pressure to the back of the paper to transfer the ink. You can buy specialist printing barrens of many varieties, but a clean wooden spoon or smooth stone also does a great job.

A selection of alternative printing barrens. Wooden spoons are brilliant.

- Textures
  A selection of textural surfaces similar to the ones used in Chapter 1. You may re-use any of those already with ink on as long as you keep the different colours of ink separate.
- Paper
  We will be hand-printing, so you need to make sure you have a lighter weight paper, maximum weight similar to basic printer paper, which is usually 80 gms. The paper will need to have a smooth surface. The heavier the paper, the harder it is to transfer the pressure from your hand through to the ink. The paper also needs to be strong so that it will not fall apart from hand-printing. Japanese washi paper between 40 gms and 80 gms is always a good bet, or lightweight cartridge. Make sure you have a few sheets to hand.
- Inking area
  If using a roller, make sure the roller width fits on the plastic and you have a nice length to roll out.
- Clean-up materials

Practise Cutting

Before undertaking this project, it is important that you feel comfortable using the tools you have and the lino you have purchased. It may be worth taking a small section of the lino and testing the tools on it so the technical use of the tool does not hinder your free expression.

How to hold the traditional tools is entirely up to how it feels comfortable and safe. As long as you are safe, those around you are safe and the tool is not being damaged then hold it how you feel comfortable. Always cut away from yourself, holding the lino steady with your spare hand. Cut steadily: there is no rush.

Never place your non-cutting hand in the path of the carving blade, hold the lino to the side or behind the blade. If wishing to cut a curved line, or a circle, then you can use your spare hand to grip the lino and turn it as you cut with your other hand. This avoids you having to turn in any awkward positions. Keep checking your cutting angle so that you remove the top surface of the lino to reveal the paler inner lino. Too deep and you just dig a hole; too shallow will risk ink filling in your cut groove and thus your cut information is lost. If using non-traditional tools, these are more free-form in technique so have a play. Scratch, hammer, scrape, sand, hit. There are many techniques that work, some will print less clearly than others. If using anything that will kick up lino dust, such as a Dremel, please wear a face mask.

Set-Up

Please make sure you have the materials as per the list and a separate inking and clean workspace. You will be working with one A5 piece of lino (approximately) so please use a knife and cutting mat to score through and cut the lino to size. It is a monochrome project. Be steady and take your time. Many small cuts without slipping are preferable to one big cut and damaging yourself. Some of the unusual tools may not respond very well to the rubber surface of the soft cut or vinyl. Please do try first.

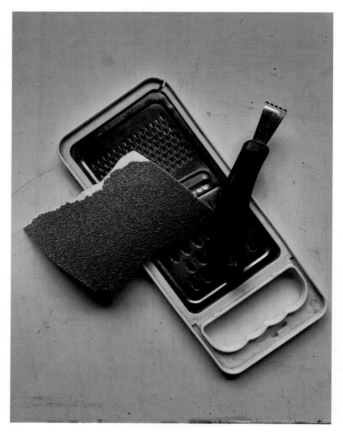
Many non-traditional carving tools can create exquisite, responsive marks.

A common holding position of the mushroom handle lino tool.

Cutting the lino steadily and away from the body and hands.

A good angle for cutting the lino is key for smooth cutting.

Turning the lino as you carve forward is a good way to cut curves.

We are going to delve straight into lino. But with no more than the bare bones of a plan. Why? Well, lino tends to be associated with lots of planning. Pencil sketches, layers, tracing, more sketches, carving, more tracing, registration, to name a few of the many processes that can stop initial expression. Here we are going to work directly onto the lino with traditional and non-traditional tools, with no pre-drawing and no working from a sketch. We will be responding to the sounds we hear around us. We will not even be looking at a scene or an object. The reason for this is to encourage you to think about what marks the tools express and thus communicate in the work; not how we can represent the world we see by creating an image, but how we can feel the expression created by the tools. By exploring this, we can begin to understand the tools and the material itself and see lino as a means of dynamic expression rather than purely a means of graphic representation, which opens many doors to expressive, unique printmaking.

Carving the Sounds

Listening to the sounds around you in your workspace, start to carve them into the lino surface. Is there a certain rhythm of the sounds that you wish to communicate? Are they soft or harsh? Looking at the tools in front of you, consider how you might use them to communicate this to the viewer. Rhythm, line, texture. Remember the areas that you carve away will be the areas that do not receive ink and therefore appear the paper colour.

Although you may be tempted to cover the whole surface of the lino, listen carefully to the sounds. There will be moments of silence (most likely), even if it is for only a few seconds. But these moments are crucial to capture, as it is with these moments that everything else sings. Leaving this empty space on the lino, be it as an unmarked area or as an area completely cut away, is a great skill to learn. Knowing when to stop mark-making and leave empty space for the image to breathe is so important. So, listen carefully for these moments and think how, when and where to include these in your lino. Some of the alternative tools may be noisy in themselves, such as a Dremel, so remember what you are wishing to record before you start carving.

Printing

Using the dolly or roller, apply a layer of ink over the surface of the lino. You are looking for an even layer of glossy ink which has a little tack when applied. Too thick and it will fill in all the fine details; too thin and it will not print an even black. For both the roller and the dolly, you want to look for a gentle hiss of ink, no big blobs or gloopy texture to the ink.

Assess your print and if you have many fine soft marks, then build up the ink layer slowly so as to avoid filling in the details with ink. If you have bolder effects, then you can go straight in with a strong layer.

Starting with a traditional lino tool to carve.

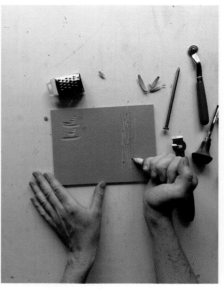
Using a sharp needle to scratch the top surface.

A grater creates some very expressive scratches.

Think when to use traditional tools for variety.

A Dremel can create fun, unpredictable textures.

Brushing off loose lino dust after the Dremel.

Lino tools can be rocked to create wiggly lines.

Using strong scissors to cut the lino intuitively.

The finished lino ready to be inked and printed.

Once you feel the lino is coated sufficiently, then place one of your pieces of paper over the surface of the inked lino. Once the paper has made contact with the ink, do not move it, as this will create a double image and appear blurry. Using the printing barren of choice, apply pressure to the back of the paper using small circular motions whilst also holding the paper in place with the spare hand. You can slip a piece of clean tissue paper between your barren and the impression paper, thus keeping the back of the paper clean. Different parts of your barren can be used to apply pressure differently. You may of course take more than one print, remembering to re-ink before taking an impression. Hand printing takes a little time to get used to, so keep practising. If you are consistently getting a faint image, then first try using a lighter weight paper. If this does not help, then next try increasing the amount of ink applied. If neither (nor a combination) of these helps, then you may just need to apply more pressure with the barren. If you are able, standing up to apply more pressure can help. The lino is capable of printing many prints so do not be afraid to try until you feel happy with your result and technique.

Setting up to ink the lino matrix with black ink.

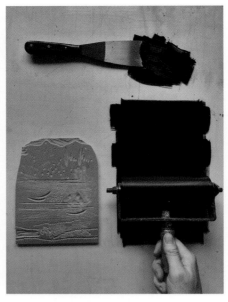
Rolling out beads of ink, creating an even surface.

Inking up the lino, creating an even, glossy layer.

The fully inked lino ready for paper and printing.

Laying the Japanese paper down onto the surface.

Using a wooden spoon to apply pressure and print.

Looking at the Marks

The marks produced by the various tools vary hugely and using the sounds as our guide, it allows the tools to develop a spontaneity that pure representational imagery would struggle to achieve. Of course, the tools and the way in which I have used them will be very different from yourself, but there are a few I would like to highlight.

Grater

The micro grater is a great tool to create scratching and scouring marks that convey a sense of energy. They are hugely satisfying to create and although they cannot be controlled in their position and edges, they can really loosen up a very tight work. If you build up the scratches, you can also completely remove the surface of the lino.

Needle

Using a needle, awl or etching needle is a very effective way to create scratch marks in the lino. You need to press firmly and really drag the tool across the surface. The results are wonderfully evocative and quite unusual. They have a tendency to fill in with thick ink layers, so it works best with a nice thin roll-up.

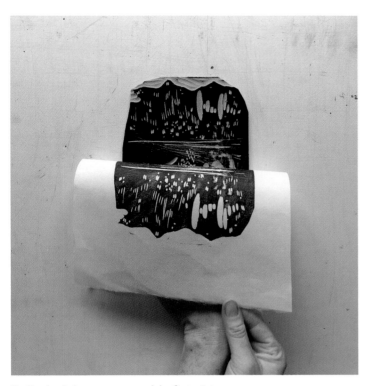

Peeling back the paper to reveal the first print.

The completed impression and the inky lino matrix.

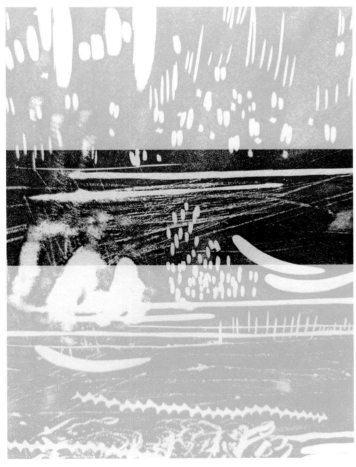

Using a grater creates some very expressive surface texture.

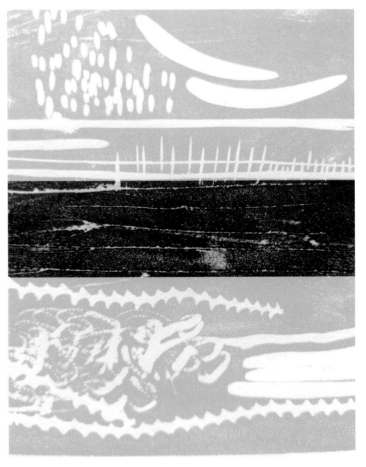

An etching needle can create some very fine scratchy lines.

Dremels are a great fun way to produce a range of textures.

Oil-based inks can be stored for years and the colour range is spectacular.

Dremel

A Dremel comes with many different interchangeable heads and many of these will create some wonderful textural effects in the lino. It is worth taking time to practise as it is a power tool and can be aggressive on the lino. It will create lino dust, so please do take suitable protective steps and wear a face mask.

DIVING INTO COLOUR

Relief prints work beautifully in monochrome as well as all the colours of the rainbow. As previously discussed, the inks used in the projects throughout the book are oil-based, and this includes the colour work. There are many new water-based inks being brought out on the market that aim to replicate the oil-based strength, but I still find nothing quite produces the same vivid tones as a traditional oil-based ink. When it comes to printing in colour, there are no set rules, just tips to be aware of. The first is to not be scared. Printmaking colours are very rich and strong and it can be quite overwhelming to know where to start. So, start with the ones you like; have a mix and play. Do not worry about colour theory, just have fun. If you are mixing colours, be cautious of the blues, reds and blacks. They

Birch Leaves, Mary Dalton. This reduction linocut was created using oil-based inks and a multitude of subtle colours.

are very strong and you would be advised to add these inks into your mix drop by drop because they can dramatically change the colour palette. White is quite chalky in printmaking, and it will aid you in mixing certain colours, but it can make colours go towards the pastel shades and sit very flat upon the paper. Again, this is not a negative thing, just something to be aware of. Never be too scared of mixing a larger quantity of ink. You will need a certain amount of ink to apply to the matrix, so there is no point in mixing a tiny dab. Colour matching an ink mix halfway through a project is possible, but not ideal, so make sure you have mixed enough. Oil-based inks will keep for a few days if covered and made airtight, so do not feel you will be wasting all the ink.

If you are mixing colour and wish to test out the mix you have made, there are two main options. The first is to use a broad palette knife and drag a line of ink down onto a clean piece of paper, preferably the paper you plan to print on. This will give you a lovely sample of how the colour will appear. This method uses a portion of your ink mix, so make sure you have enough.

The second method is the finger dab. Using a clean finger (or clean rag over a finger), take a small blob of your ink mix and dab it onto a piece of paper using circular motions outwards. In essence, you will end up with almost a flower effect of a strong middle and graduating tones heading outwards. With experience you will begin to understand what part of the tonal range best represents the effect of the impression you will be taking.

Using a broad palette knife to drag down the colour.

The finished palette knife colour test.

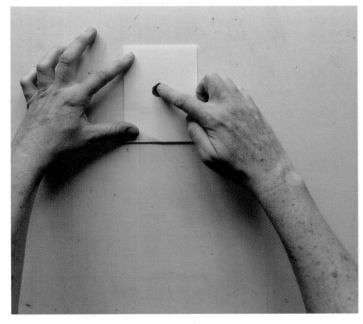

Using a clean finger to dab out the test ink.

The finished finger dab colour test.

A COLOURFUL SILHOUETTE

Having had a delve into the spontaneous effects of lino, let's now explore how we can combine these with other relief methods, and take that jump into glorious colour. The next project will require the same set up as before, but you are also going to be working in colour so please make sure that you have a big enough area to roll out two colours of your choice plus monochrome. Of course, each colour may be cleaned up sequentially as we use them to reduce this dependency on space. This project does include a very basic registration technique. It is quick and does not require any set up of boards, thus allowing one to test the print and play.

To highlight how colour and bold lino can completely transform an impression, we will be developing the stencil image created in the 'Making A Print' project in Chapter 1. If you have already made this print, you may use it or make a new one as you wish. You will also need a new piece of lino that is bigger than your stencilled impression. It is important that the lino is cut with edges square.

The relief print from Chapter 1 will be developed in this project.

After you have made a print from the 'Making A Print' project, your workspace needs to be prepared for rolling up colour and lino cutting. Using the lino and your tools of choice, including those unusual ones you discovered earlier, start creating a pattern upon the lino. Use the tools for mark-making rather than representing the window, doors, flowers that might be surrounding you. The pattern may be rhythmical and repeated in formation across the lino surface, or more lucid and free-form. Perhaps gain inspiration for the marks of one of the textures that is in the object silhouette print? Enjoy the carving.

When complete, you will need to create a paper mask to cover up your little object impression before printing the lino. This can be done with thin tissue or newsprint and placed gently over the object. You can use a tiny amount of light tack masking tape to pin down the mask at an edge. Roll out your first colour of choice, ink up your lino and place the lino ink side down onto your paper in the position you wish. Next, slide the paper and lino to the workspace edge and flip the two over gently so that you may hand print the impression from the back. This is a quick method of registration that means you do not need to set up a registration board. The tackiness of the ink should be enough to initially stick the paper to the lino, allowing you to flip it over. Print your lino.

Once printed, gently peel away the paper, keeping the paper mask in place if you can. Using a little oil and a clean rag, wipe your lino clean of the first ink colour. Make sure no oil has pooled in the carved recesses. Clean up and roll out your second colour and ink the lino. Make sure you have the mask over your object and then lay the lino down again on the paper but this time, you need to turn the lino through 180 degrees, so the top is the bottom and the bottom the top. Align the lino in position with the previous layer by eye and flip over and print. This registration by eye method is actually very good training. You may not always have registration devices to hand, so let's start with the basic method. The simple 180-degree turn of the lino will create unexpected pattern formations that add a dynamic energy to the print.

EXPERIMENTATION TO CHALLENGE FURTHER

It is already very clear to see the numerous possibilities with relief work. Additionally, this relief work need not be repetitive, but very individual and energetic. We have not even looked at reduction or multi-plate work, which can add a further dimension, allowing the creator to express further. The following examples are like little doors into a world of further relief techniques that you are able to pursue and integrate into work as you wish.

Using traditional tools to carve patterns and marks on lino.

Placing a thin paper mask over the printed object impression.

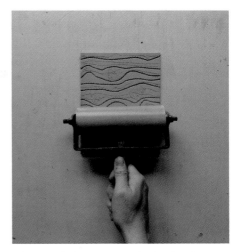

Inking up the lino matrix with a bright primrose yellow ink.

Placing the inked lino in position on the impression paper.

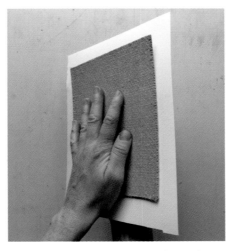

Carefully gripping and flipping the lino and paper together.

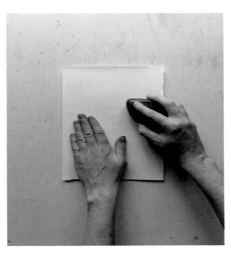

Hand printing the inked lino using a wooden hand-held barren.

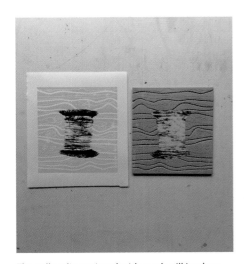

The yellow lino printed with mask still in place over object.

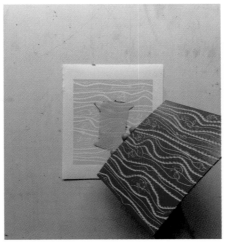

Printing the red lino next, rotating the matrix by 180 degrees.

The final impression with the mask removed from the object.

Hung Up Trees (Birch), Mary Dalton. This print is a unique reduction linocut, printed in over twenty layers of reduction and colour work.

The three separate lino matrices with carving ready for ink.

Reduction Relief Work

When you hear mention of 'reduction' linocut, this is describing a lino matrix that has been carved, inked and printed, then cleaned, carved further, inked and printed in register on top of the first impression. This process of carving and printing with the same matrix may continue until there is no more lino left. The same principles apply to woodcut or any other matrix with reduction potential. When working in this manner, if you wish for your marks to be in register you will need to set up a registration system or register by eye. Chapter 10 has information on the various options for this. The key with any registration

The impression from carved lino inked and printed in yellow.

The lino is carved further, then printed in red on the yellow.

Finally, the lino is carved more and printed in blue on top.

The impression taken when all three are printed in register.

The prints taken from the three matrices printed separately.

system is to find one that works for you and the project and to stick with it throughout. Changing system halfway through can be difficult. Reduction work can open up many possibilities of colour work and complex, bold images.

Multi-Plate Work

Multi-plate relief work describes a print created from more than one matrix, printed in sequence on the same impression. The multi-plate method means you do not need to stick with the same matrix; thus, colours and forms can be overlaid in different shapes more readily rather than staying in the reduction register. You can also create different types of relief plates and print them in the same impression, for example a linocut combined with woodcut overprinted with a home-made cork stamp.

Lino as a Stamping Surface

Using the stamping textures we have explored, we can transfer these onto the surface of the lino directly and then transfer to the paper impression. Why? Well, if I carve a shape into lino, I can then stamp inked textures directly onto the lino surface, all of which will be kept within the crisp borders of the original graphic linocut. It is a bold and direct way of introducing texture without having to carve the lino, thus allowing for more opportunity to carve further into the lino at a later date.

Custom Matrix

If you are interested in creating a matrix from specific textures, which you will re-use, then you are able to. It is as simple as gluing down your chosen textures onto a piece of grey board. It is quite important that the textures are of a similar depth so that you are able to ink them evenly. This matrix will need to be sealed with shellac or another tough, waterproof varnish. If you wish to print onto damp paper with these printing plates, if the glue is not sealed with a waterproof varnish it will stick to your damp paper when running under a press. If you are wishing to print by hand, this stage is less imperative, and you can simply apply ink to the top surface and hand print or stamp. This method begins to delve into collagraph. It is a very useful process to know because some of the more organic textures you can achieve work beautifully with a more graphic medium, such as lino. You can even replace the grey board with cut timber sheeting to make it sturdier and easier to stamp.

Wallpaper Rollers

If you have any old cheap printmaking rollers around they can be transformed into a relief surface to create repeat pattern on prints. In days gone by, wallpaper was sometimes printed using carved wooden rollers, similar to giant rolling pins. These would be inked up and run across the length of the

Inking up the texture you wish to apply to the lino surface.

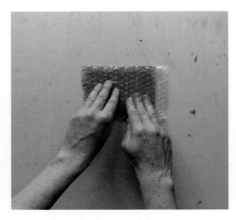

Pressing down the ink side of the texture onto the cut lino.

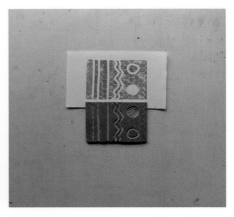

The completed print of the carved lino with texture applied.

Using PVA glue to stick down textures onto the grey board.

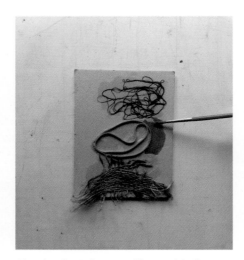

After the glue is dry, several layers of shellac are applied.

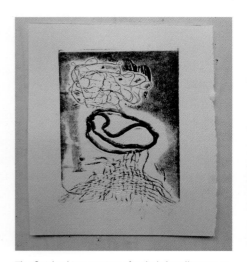

The finished impression after lightly rolling up in black ink.

Fantastic collagraph people made on a pop-up printmaking session run by the Washroom Pop-Up Press.

wallpaper, creating a repeat pattern. If you do not have any old printmaking rollers, as an alternative you can also cover rolling pins or similar tough tubes. You will need to seal your textured roller to make it last longer. Many people use shellac, but you can also roll the unsealed roller through a layer of oil-based ink, let this dry, and it will act as a decent seal for a period of time. These rollers are brilliant to create a bold gestural repeat texture, especially if combined with the use of masks as in the second project. Be aware that the ink will fade as you roll, so you either need to accept this and integrate it as part of the work, or re-ink and start rolling again from the same point. A little notch or mark on the edge of the roller can act as a useful guide to know when to stop rolling and to return to the same point.

Barren Pressure

Up until now, we have been attempting to create an even impression across the surface of our relief matrix. This has been done using a wooden spoon or similar hand-printing barren. However, you can be more adventurous in your pressure application when printing. If you use the end of your wooden spoon to apply pressure in squiggles or lines, you will get a completely different impression. This technique can be extended further using different tools to apply pressure and the results can be beautiful and unusual.

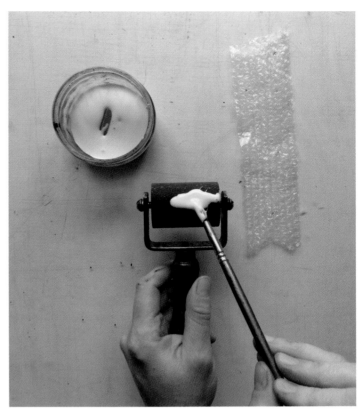

Apply a strong glue to the roller's surface using a brush.

The materials required to make a basic repeat roller pattern.

Cut your material to size and stick onto the roller's surface.

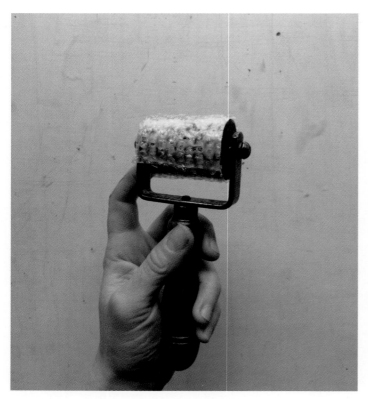

Trim the overlap neatly and leave to dry well before using.

Once dry, the roller can be inked up to create a repeat pattern.

Barren pressure can completely change the atmosphere of a relief print. Note here the squiggles created using the pointy end of a wooden spoon to hand print. The dark stripes were printed by using the flat end of the bowl of the wooden spoon to apply pressure in streaks.

HYBRID RELIEF PRINT

The techniques we have covered in this chapter offer you an insight into the possibilities of relief printing. A print can really sing when different techniques are used in combination to express to the viewer the complexity of the moment being captured. In some cases, this may only be two different relief techniques; in others it may be many, many more. It is down to the artist to pick and choose which suits the needs of the time. It will come to a stage in making works where the technique comes easily and does not hinder the full flow of creation. This will come with time and practice and lots of fun experiments along the way.

PROJECT

A WINDOW VIEW

The following project will be using a minimum of three different relief methods. It is designed as a follow along, but not one to replicate. You should choose your own subject and materials but use this project here as a guide to keep you on track and attentive to the various techniques being executed. In this project, I am expressing a scene in our garden which can be easily viewed from the studio window. The outdoor scene enables a complex array of texture and shape to be communicated in the final print, thus acting as an interesting challenge for the artist to get the balance of texture and empty space.

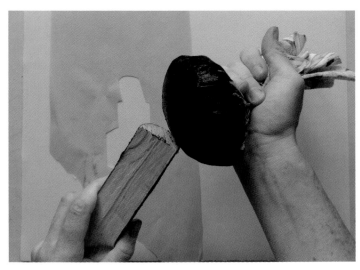

Using the dolly to apply ink to the first textures to print.

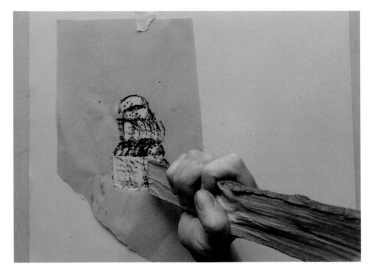

Hand stamping the initial texture through a silhouette mask.

The first shape printed and revealed when a mask is removed.

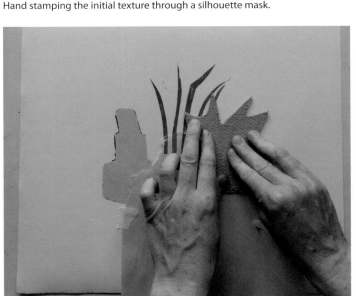

Using masks to protect areas prior to printing a lino stamp.

Building up the foliage with colours and textures of leaves.

Using alternative tools to add bold line in the white space.

Add dynamic, bright marks to keep the image alive and fluid.

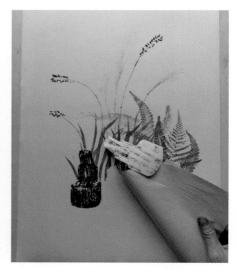

Removing the mask when ready to print the next layer on top.

Adding lino stamps to the foreground, introducing bold shape.

Adding a contrasting colour to the work changes the dynamic.

Using a bright and unexpected colour to add the final marks.

The complete work demonstrates what can be achieved by hand.

THE JOURNEY IS ENDLESS

Relief work is hugely accessible and used by many artists who may not consider printmaking to be their primary expression. As we have seen from the hybrid relief project above, relief impressions can be taken from pretty much any surface and can be hand stamped to great effect. Thus they become a huge textural asset to many artistic media.

It is wonderful to see how artists can engage so directly with the hand-printing methods to produce glorious relief prints. There is nothing at all to be ashamed of in using hand stamping methods: they are powerful, evocative, and most definitely print-making. You can of course translate the principles of cutting lino to cutting wood. The effects are different, and it is a whole new world to explore, from the Japanese methods of wood cutting to those artists who scavenge timber from skips and work on a huge scale.

Sometimes with relief work it requires thinking outside the box. Slabs of solid plaster of Paris can be carved and inked up to produce wonderful textured and stony-looking prints. They have a specific quality amongst relief printmaking that is very beautiful. As with all these techniques in printmaking, the more you explore, the more you find. It is a great journey to start on and the information in this chapter should put you in a good position to feel confident to explore further techniques.

Water Spirit Puppet, Mary Dalton. Plaster cast printing is hugely fun and another way to generate an impression from relief textures. This is discussed further in Chapter 9.

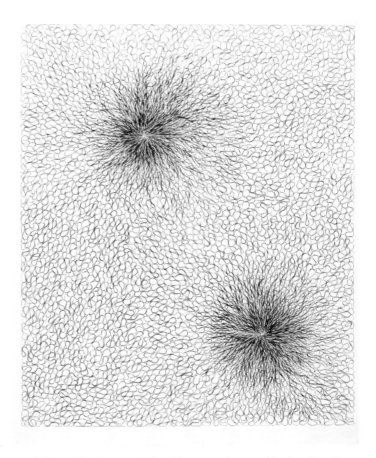

Untitled, 2006, Tara Donovan, ink on Kozo paper from a rubber band matrix, 55" × 42" (139.7cm × 106.7cm). (Photo: Kerry Ryan McFate, courtesy Pace Gallery © Tara Donovan)

CHAPTER 3

SPONTANEOUS MONOCHROMES IN A SINGLE PULL

Working in monochrome can encourage you to think about form and texture. Printmaking has a huge history of working in black and white and it is still a popular choice amongst contemporary printmakers. It is bold, graphic, and accentuates the wonderful array of texture and form found in the multitude of printmaking techniques. To keep it energetic and full of spontaneous marks can sometimes be a challenge; all the more reason to explore techniques that loosen you up to enable a more dynamic approach. In this chapter we will explore approaches to working in monochrome that will allow for a fluid approach to expression, all generating impressions in a single pull. Approaches will include both hand printing and the use of an etching press, and we will explore how these affect the result. Working with a single pull encourages a result that produces a spontaneous and lively monochrome print.

WHAT IS A MONOPRINT?

A monoprint simply translates as a single (mono) print. Thus, it covers any print that is not editioned and is unique. This book places a great emphasis on the production of unique prints, in essence monoprints. Some of the techniques used to create those unique prints, such as the use of lino, are more conventionally used as part of an editioned print. However, we are using them for their unique expression, which thus creates a unique print. In this chapter the techniques explored cannot be editioned because we will not be creating a permanent matrix. The matrix is something that will be created specifically for each print and thus cannot be reproduced exactly. A monoprint sits under the category of a planographic print.

The artist Jemma Gunning working on a large-scale monoprint.

This means that all the ink information sits on a singular plane on the matrix. There is no carving, nor recesses, in the matrix.

Why a Single Pull?

A 'pull' in printmaking describes the impression paper being pulled away from the printing matrix after it has been printed. A single pull means that the completed impression has generated

Snowdonia, Jemma Gunning. A beautiful example of an expressive single pull monoprint. The layering and gestural marks give the work life and energy.

all its textures, layers and marks through just one pull; there have been no further additions after that first pull. When working with alternative techniques, many of them rely upon the building of layers and creating the work through many processes. The single pull seems counter-intuitive to this process, but in fact by exploring this manner of working, you generate great confidence, life and energy that then feeds further into other processes. Working with single pull prints also means that there is very little space to hide mistakes in. Everything has to be done with conviction and a knowledge of the process, which comes through having fun with the prints and learning at every turn when things did not turn out as expected.

Monoprint Monochromes

Many unique prints embrace the more spontaneous element of printmaking, which makes them very dynamic and alive. When working in monochrome, it can be tempting to just work in a singular layer with one technique, because the result will still look satisfying and graphically appealing. However, monochrome images may be developed in a multitude of layers that incorporate many techniques, from relief work to direct drawing, from collage to stamping, all of which can be layered and printed in a single pull. It is all about understanding the balance of when to introduce the technique and what it can offer the artist.

We will be working with hand printing techniques as well as utilizing a printing press. Both options offer different effects and possibilities for the artist, and can even be combined. It is important to keep an open mind and embrace the unexpected when working with the following projects.

Materials

For this chapter's projects, you will need:

- Sheet of plastic
  The plastic is used in several projects as a surface onto which we will apply ink to then create a matrix. It should be approximately A4 or the size you wish to create images and 3–8 mm in depth. Do not go too tiny, as the lack of space will end up hindering expression. The plastic will be going under a press, so it is important it is not glass as this will potentially crack under the pressure. If plastic is not accessible, you can also use the shiny side of a cereal packet. The plastic can be cleaned and re-used multiple times.
- Mirror
- Black ink
- Palette knife, roller/dolly
- Wooden spoon or other printing barren
- Inking area and clean printing area
- Etching press (This is not essential for all the projects, but it is for some. *See* Chapter 10 for more information on presses.)

A few of the specific tools needed for the projects in this chapter.

- Paper
  Paper to print on needs to be lightweight (around 40–80 gms) for hand-printing and heavier weight (cartridge and up to 220 gms printing paper) for the press work. A selection of paper fitting this category is perfect. You will also need some scrap paper for mask making and clean tissue paper for protection of prints.
- Tetra Pak
  From fruit juice cartons, long life milk or similar. You may also use cereal packet card as it has a similar plastic-coated surface. Make sure the packaging is flat packed, clean and dry.
- Household materials
- Black water-soluble crayon

PROJECT

STARTING WITH BLACK: NEGATIVE LINE

Working in monochrome in this chapter entails two main tones: black ink and white paper. The grey tonal range in between may appear grey to the human eye, but it is still just made from black ink that has been manipulated to give the appearance of a tonal range. There has been no mixing of black and white ink to make grey. Various techniques can be employed to introduce a basic tonal range, and we will look at a few of these in this project.

Tonal work can be created using monochrome techniques, not by mixing up grey ink.

Set-Up

This project will get inky, so please make sure that you have a suitable area to work in, and protective clothing for yourself. You will need your piece of plastic and your inking area set up with a roll-up of black ink. You will also need your selection of household textures and alternative drawing materials. If using a press, you will need to set it up to receive the depth of the plastic matrix safely. If not using a press, you will need your hand printing barren. Make sure your paper is slightly bigger than your plastic matrix, or if not, you are aware of your paper size when creating your print. If using a press, printing on damp paper will help pick up details so make sure you are prepared to do this.

The inspiration for the imagery on this project is yourself: a dreaded self-portrait. But do not worry, since the strong lines and marks we will be creating for the face will actually negate the fact it may not look anything like you! The portrait is a great way to showcase the tonal values and bold textures that can be

created from this technique. You will be working into a fully black ink background, using your tools to remove ink, creating a negative line. This means that when you print the image, the areas that have been removed will reveal the paper colour (white), thus creating a negative space against the positive black areas. The ink background can be applied with a roller, the easiest, or with your dolly by just working your way across spreading the ink out with little circular motions. The ink needs to be of a slight tack: a nice even gloss but not so thick that any mark you make immediately fills back in on itself.

Printing

If printing under a press, place the plastic matrix down first and damp paper on top and then run through. Remember to set the pressure of the press according to the depth of your plastic. You may need runners to help; please refer to Chapter 10 for instructions to how to use these correctly. If printing by hand, place dry lightweight paper on top of your plastic and hold securely in place with your non-printing hand. Using the barren, apply

Hand rolling out an even and light gloss layer of black ink.

The plastic is evenly covered, and light can barely penetrate.

Using a finger and a rag to remove the black ink to add tone.

A rag can be used with other tools, creating different marks.

Using unusual tools to remove ink can generate fun textures.

Dragging grey board to remove top layers of ink, adding tone.

Scraping a palette knife along the ink adds movement to the hair.

Using a pointed tool can add smaller details before printing.

Printing the drawing under an etching press using damp paper.

The completed print shows the full range of marks generated.

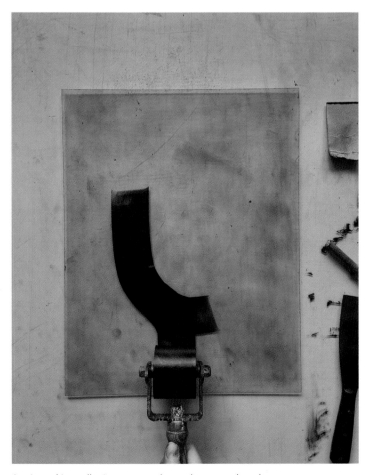

A printmaking roller is a great tool to make gestural marks.

pressure all over in small firm circular motions. A wooden spoon is great for this. If you can, use the smooth surface of the wooden spoon, not the edge. The edge will apply more high pressure in a point, thus creating some uneven print marks. They are interesting and we will look at this shortly, but right now we are attempting an even impression.

The resultant print has a great range of marks and textures. The solid black background allows the image to pop out and it creates atmospheric impression.

PROJECT

STARTING WITH WHITE – POSITIVE TEXTURE

Using the same set-up as the previous project, this print will start to demonstrate how techniques from previous chapters may be integrated. In order to act as a technical comparison, we will use the self-portrait again as the starting point. This time, you do not need to roll up a black background, as you will be applying black ink to your clean sheet of plastic. Make sure your plastic sheet from the previous project is thoroughly cleaned and dried before commencing this one. If you wish, you may also bring in scraps of cut lino texture or stamps from the previous chapters to use in this project.

A roller can generate a range of effects for a bold outline.

Scraping on thick layers of ink is great for abstract form.

Using alternative tools to remove ink adds areas of detail.

It is good to build up in layers, from detail to broad marks.

String and other objects can be inked up to transfer texture.

Stamping inked texture down using newspaper as a protection.

The completed image built of a range of marks ready to print.

Printing the image under an etching press using damp paper.

The print communicates the energy of the autographic marks.

USING POSITIVE AND NEGATIVE IN HARMONY

As you will have experienced and seen from the two projects, creating positive and negative textures and tones not only generates a different end result, but it also encourages the artist to approach the subject matter differently. So how can we pull the strengths from both and move them forward in harmony?

The following techniques are ways to use certain tools to create both positive and negative marks that work together and expressively. There are numerous ways to approach monoprint, the key being to allow the spontaneity of the tool to guide you, whilst also making sure that you are aware of the balance of the empty space and the more complex areas.

Rags

Rags are used by many artists in monoprint. They can be used to remove areas of ink or to apply ink. They can be scrunched, twisted, wrapped round a finger, dabbed and wiped. Used in combination with another tool they can also generate a range of expressive marks. For instance, a rag-covered knitting needle will draw a softer line then a knitting needle left bare. Rags are brilliant at both removing and adding ink, so have fun using them to do both in the same impression. They can get inky very quickly, but you can leave them to dry naturally and then re-use them somewhat. If removing large areas of ink with a rag, use a dirty one first to get rid of the bulk of the ink, and then use the clean one to remove the last of the ink. If you wish to remove all the ink from an area, then a small amount of vegetable oil on a rag helps loosen the ink and wipe it off completely.

Snowdonia (detail), Jemma Gunning. The layering and use of tools is key to bringing a single pull print together. Here we can see a stunning use of movement and processes to allow the positive and negative spaces to work in harmony.

Using a clean rag to wipe clean an area of solid black ink.

The area wiped clean communicates the energy of the gesture.

The rag scrunched, dipped in ink, and dabbed onto the matrix.

A knitting needle wrapped in rag removing soft lines of ink.

Two tissue paper masks added before printing to add contrast.

The test print illustrates the mark-making range of one rag.

The crayon is used to draw directly on the plastic's surface.

It can be used for line work and shading, as well as smudged.

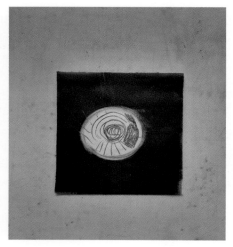

The print showing the different tones of the crayon and ink.

Rags are great at creating a visual blend, as they can soften harsh edges and thus combine the positive and negative spaces beautifully. They are also brilliant at adding texture to large areas that contain no ink. You can use them in combination with a mask to really emphasize forms.

Water-Based Crayons

These crayons are readily available and very useful. It is important to note that the use of them relies upon working with damp paper to create your impression. If you are hand printing, you can dampen your paper before printing. You will need to place a piece of clean tissue paper between the back of the damp paper and your printing barren so as to not ruck up the damp paper fibres with the rubbing pressure. You will also need to print quickly to avoid the paper drying up. It is all possible, and when you see the possibilities with the crayon, well worth it.

The crayon being used in this chapter is just black, but they do come in a full range of colours. The crayon is used like a drawing tool to apply positive marks into the negative spaces. But because it looks and feels like an autographic mark, it has a wonderful way of linking the positive and negative spaces of a print. The black crayon prints much lighter than a printing ink black, more akin to a soft charcoal grey. This tonal change is useful to add movement and energy to a print that may be too uniform.

Brush Marks

The viscosity of oil-based ink describes the amount of oil in the ink. The more oil, the looser the ink; the less oil, the tackier the ink. If you add a few drops of oil to a basic black ink mix (about a 50p-sized blob) and mix well, you will notice it will get glossier and looser. This more viscose ink will allow you to generate a longer base of ink, which means it will spread out further, more easily and fluidly. Printing ink can be very stiff, but by increasing the viscosity, you can generate the right consistency to allow you to paint and create more fluid spontaneous black marks. This allows you to introduce a great energy of positive marks into negative spaces, as well as being able to smear and wipe away those more viscose areas of black ink more fluidly.

Some artists will use a solvent to loosen the oil base ink, such as white spirit. This is of course possible, but I try to avoid the use of such solvents wherever possible and look for alternative

Adding drops of thin copper plate reducing oil to loosen the ink.

Use a paintbrush or another gestural tool to 'paint' marks.

The tester range of marks ready to print using damp paper.

The print communicating the fluid, spontaneous marks made.

solutions. Using the oil as a loosening agent does still mean the ink is tacky rather than completely 'wet,' but it does offer you a chance to create more fluid marks.

Subtle Layers

Achieving a sense of depth in a spontaneous monochrome print can be very tricky, because of the nature of working only with the black and white spaces. However, the following technique can help a little to create a sense of spatial depth. If you have created an ink mark that you actually wish to appear further back in the image, then simply take a piece of clean tissue paper and lay it over the ink and gently remove some of the ink by rubbing with your finger. This will just knock back that strong black and allow you to then add further richer positive marks on top. This can be repeated further if you wish for an even softer background mark. It is a great way to add gentle positive information in a negative space, without it appearing to dominate.

True-Grain

True-Grain is a plastic film commonly used in photo lithography and other photo-exposure methods. It has a grain added

Using tissue paper to pat off and remove the top ink layers.

Peeling back the tissue shows how much ink has been removed.

Applying a freshly inked stamp atop the area with less ink.

The print showing the darker areas of fresh marks against the grey tone.

to one side, which replicates a dpi matrix, and it is this grain that allows you to draw, paint and mark-make freely onto its surface. The micro grain added means that water-based media do not pool and even washes can be generated alongside the use of oil-based media.

It is useful in this instance as a matrix onto which you create your marks. If you use the water-based wax crayon, you will notice it is more sensitive to the texture of the marks than plain plastic. Additionally, you may create wash effects with water and the crayon (or even watercolours), let this dry and print onto damp paper, creating a beautiful, layered image. You may combine both the water-based techniques and traditional oil-based printing ink onto one matrix. If you wish to recreate the subtlety of the washes, then it is best to print under an etching press at high pressure. If you do use water-based media in your impression, you will not be able to add any other subsequent layers upon the impression that require to be printed with damp paper. If you dampen the paper, your wonderful water-based marks will run. The film is cleaned with vegetable oil or water (depending on the medium used) and may be re-used many times.

Barren Pressure

If you have been hand printing, you will notice that any change in pressure through the printing barren can affect the mark created on the impression. The use of a wooden spoon tip rather than the smooth outside head can create some interesting effects and it is certainly worth exploring this further. If you wish to have some input upon the texture of the final impression, then altering how you hand print is very useful. It is an open-ended path, with approaches ranging from using a stick through to your fingers to apply pressure through the paper and pick up ink. It works very well if using it in combination with more solid areas of impression. Note, that if you print a single pull under a press, then this option is not possible since the press is designed to generate an even pressure all over. So in this instance, hand printing is the best and only option.

GETTING THE TETRA-PAK OUT

Tetra-pak is a plastic-coated card, so in essence the plastic side may be used in a similar fashion to the plastic matrix we have already used. The major advantage is that it can be cut up or torn into a wonderful array of different pieces that may be subsequently laid out on the press bed to create a more free-form approach to printmaking.

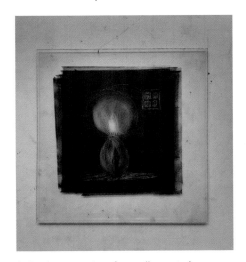
A simple monoprint of a candle created on a plastic surface.

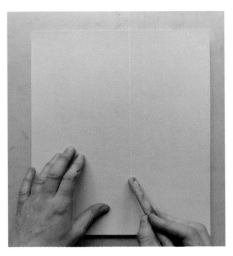
Using the end of the wooden spoon to apply specific pressure.

The print given life and dynamics using hand printing.

All the processes that we have currently used may also be applied to the Tetra Pak, from inking it black and removing marks through to stamping. There is also one further technique relevant to this chapter that is unique to the Tetra Pak. If you scratch the surface of the Tetra Pak to create incised lines, you can then roll over the top with a thin layer of black ink. The black ink sits only on the surface and does not penetrate the incised lines. The resultant print reveals your scratched marks as white and the background as black. It allows you to generate some very strong graphic textures, especially if you experiment with the tool with which you incise the surface.

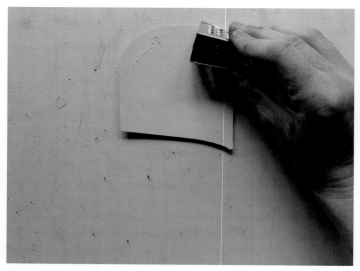

Making incised marks on the surface of some Tetra Pak using a grater.

Rolling over with a thin layer of black ink revealing the negative marks.

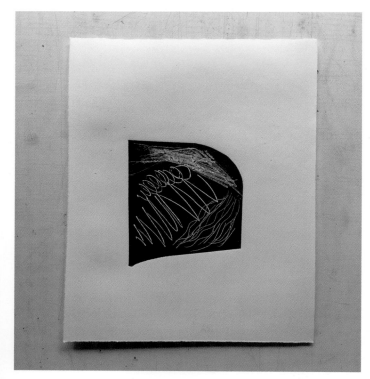

The completed impression is bold and fun – a great use of Tetra Pak.

PROJECT

TETRA PAK COLLAGE

This following micro-project is a great introduction to the spontaneity that can happen with collage and print. Make sure you have a carton of approximately 1 litre in size, cleaned and flattened out to the net. We will still need black ink and all the print materials you will have used in the first two projects. You will also need to ink up your plastic sheet with black ink, as you did in the first positive mark-making exercise. This project may – at a push – be hand printed, but works best under an etching press printed with damp paper.

There is no theme for this project; see it as a doodle. If it is becoming difficult to find inspiration, do not panic. A great way to embrace the imagination and to let the marks freely flow is to use scissors as your drawing tool. Get your Tetra Pak and cut it into pieces, no smaller than a 50p piece. Generate a full range of shapes and sizes you like. Perhaps take inspiration from silhouettes around you in your workspace. Once you have done this, you may already feel a little liberated from the long-life milk carton that was in front of you. Next, add ink marks to half of the pieces you have cut up. These marks can be made

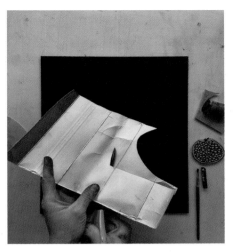

A clean, dry Tetra Pak carton is cut up for small segments.

Each segment is worked separately to create a range of marks.

Old lino can be used to stamp texture directly on the pieces.

Work directly on the plastic whilst constructing the pieces.

Stamping onto the plastic gives you options for more layers.

Using masked forms allows you to be bold with negative space.

Fine line detail is added near the end as a finishing touch.

The completed abstract print with a range of dynamic layers.

from anything: scrunched newspaper dipped in ink, your finger-prints, water-based crayon, incised lines. It is purely to generate a texture. You can also ink up the pieces in solid black and work into them as with the first project, removing areas of ink. Once completed, these segments can be laid out in any position you wish upon the inked-up plastic sheet on your press bed. Shapes and imagery will soon begin to appear, or if not, at least you will have a beautiful pattern arrangement you can play with. You will still have half the Tetra Pak pieces unmarked, so now you can integrate these into the image, and assess what marks you wish to make on them having already started the work on the others. This process should allow you to be guided by your imagination and by your spontaneity.

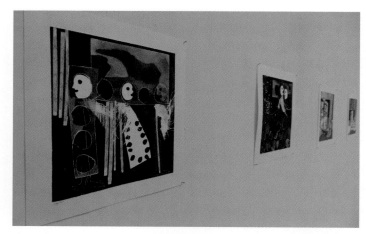

Untitled (series), Mary Dalton. Photographer: AB. Single pull monochromes work well if printed in series; their stories feed into one another and this gives them a unity across several impressions.

LEARNING AND DEVELOPING FROM A SPONTANEOUS START

Printmaking by its nature has many techniques that can hinder the artist being truly spontaneous. Monoprint and these methods we have been looking at are very direct and intuitive. It can sometimes take some getting used to, especially if you are new to ink, rollers and presses, but it is worth pursuing. Creating images that develop directly through time from the imagination offer much inspiration for future development. More often than not they too also become works in their own right, holding their strength because of their directness and energy. When working in this very quick and free manner, it is easy to cut corners on keeping paper clean, or making sure you have the right press pressure. It is important to stay in control of these minor technical aspects, however, because you never know which of the prints sing to you and you wish to keep. A black fingerprint in the wrong place can really have an effect on an image. Have a look at Chapter 10 for tips on good printmaking habits, so they become second nature and you do not even worry about them.

The further you delve into these techniques, the more you will begin to think in a multi-disciplinary way, and bring in an element of linocut, or stamping, or embossing. This method of single pull working often happens sequentially, so make sure you give yourself time and space to anticipate making a series as you get into the flow of things. Drawing upon what we have looked at thus far, I have highlighted a few techniques to integrate and challenge, that are well worth playing with.

The Elusive Rich Black

Black is like a printmaker's bread and butter. Every printer will have a favourite, and the list of variants is pretty long. And they do all have their place and their different nuances. Before one even delves into the extensive list of black inks, it is a skill in itself to be able to get a rich black background consistently across your prints. This background is used in the instances where you start with a black inky matrix and subsequently remove areas back to white. If you leave some areas of this black background as a solid black, it can be so frustrating to pull the print only to find the solid, rich black you were expecting is mottled and a bit disappointing. Attempting to get a rich black with the thin layers of ink we have been using may be difficult to achieve with a hand-printing barren, so if you are after the solid black, it would be best to gain access to a press. I have a few tips which can increase the chances of consistently getting the black solid and rich; however, it does also take practice and knowing your tools. But that is OK, it means more printing!

Firstly, if using a press, make sure it is at the right pressure. It needs to be set tight, similar to an etching plate pressure. Set your pressure for the depth of matrix you are using, and if this means resetting the press you may need to do so. Chapter 10 has further information on how to do this.

Secondly, make sure you are printing on evenly dampened paper. The spray or sponge technique works well enough for quick printing and generating ideas, but if you feel you are creating a series you wish to celebrate, then pre-soaking and preparing a damp paper stack in advance does make a difference. This is discussed in Chapter 10.

Thirdly, a hard rubber roller is best for applying a nice even layer. The dolly does and can work, but if you wish for consistency, a roller is best. Communal studios will have ones you can use. Make sure you choose one which has the most even surface, so no lumps of old ink or scratches as this can affect your roll-up. The ink you are using needs to be free of bits and the roll-up completely smooth. Apply three lines of ink to create an efficient and even roll-up. Roll out evenly, letting the roller spin off the surface occasionally to generate an even spread of ink. You

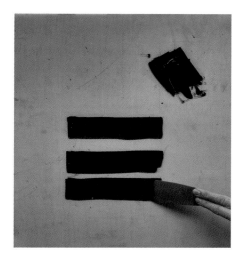
Apply three even beads of ink on your roll-up surface.

Using a good quality hard rubber roller, roll out evenly.

Any detritus on the roller or in the ink can be removed.

Roll out evenly onto your plastic matrix.

You can check for ink levels and evenness.

should be able to spot any bits as you roll out. Remove them with the edge of a scrap of thick paper and place to the side. Your ink needs to be a nice gloss, but not tacky or look all blobby. A nice gentle hiss needs to be heard.

Finally, rolling out is crucial. Make sure you roll out evenly and build up the layers by recharging your roller frequently. Recharging describes returning your roller to your roll-up surface to gather more fresh ink. If your roller is smaller in width then the matrix, you will need to roll from different directions to prevent tram lines, rotating your matrix if need be. Tram lines are the lines created by the edge of rollers where a bit more ink gathers and it leaves a darker line. These become more obvious in lighter colours, but can be still visible in blacks. You are looking to achieve a glossy black surface on your matrix. Light should not penetrate when holding it up to a light. When you draw into it with a tool, the drawn line should not fill in with more ink; it should remain visible and clean. You do not want a gathering of ink either side of the drawn line since this will fill in your drawn mark under the pressure of the press.

Masks

Mask-making will recur in various forms throughout this book as it is a very useful element in creating many dynamic prints. We have already looked at it and used it in the previous chapters,

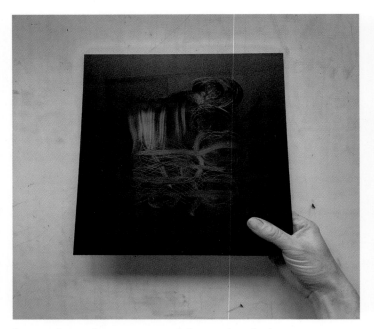

An example negative monotype matrix is created on plastic.

Paper forms are laid down onto the surface and it is printed.

The printed paper shapes are carefully peeled away and kept.

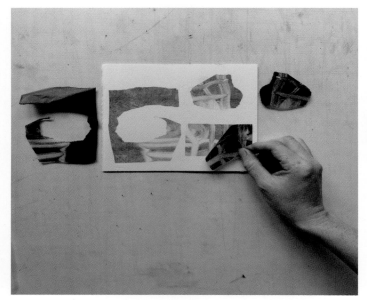

The shapes are printed ink side down onto impression paper.

and its application in this chapter is similar. Bold masks are a great way to create strong forms within the image. If using a black inky background, it is worth testing the paper you plan to use for the mask, as some paper will allow the ink to seep through. When you print with a mask, you will also notice that the back of the mask which has been in contact with the ink on the matrix will have some wonderful textures on it. This can be used in subsequent prints as a way of generating a lighter toned texture. If using oil-based ink, the ink on the paper will stay usable for an hour or so before the paper absorbs it all.

Playing with the Blind Emboss

Blind embossing is a great way to introduce a texture into the white space that is subtle yet can also be dramatic in its contrast to the rest of the image. Any flat items may be used under a printing press to create an emboss. It is crucial that you are aware of the item's thickness; adjust the pressure accordingly so that it does not damage the press or the blankets. Be very careful of using metal items to create an emboss because they have no 'give' in them and they risk damaging your press and blankets. Metal wire, chicken wire, cutlery and all such items should be absolutely avoided for press work. Generally, if unsure of the suitability of a metal item, it is advisable to find an alternative. You can also very successfully hand emboss items.

Embossing tends to work better on a medium to heavy weight pulp paper. The paper will take on a better impression of the embossed items if there is more paper weight for it to 'sink' into. A lightweight Japanese paper will struggle to take an emboss.

If wishing to integrate an emboss into an area of white on an already printed impression, this is entirely possible. Once you have printed your impression, you can re-dampen your paper and run it under the press with your embossing texture. You

are also able to run the emboss through at the same time as an inked matrix, in a single pull. On both accounts, it is advisable to change your felt blankets to an old set or even a piece of foam to prevent the embossing transferring to your good set of printing blankets.

If hand printing, you will need to place your emboss item underneath dry paper and using a blunt tool such as a rounded crochet hook or bookbinder's bone, very gently apply pressure and work the paper around the emboss. You can also buy specific hand embossing tools for this purpose.

Playing with the material on the impression for placement.

The completed emboss adds textural interest to the impression.

Laying the impression paper in place on top of the material.

Using a blunt tool to hand emboss a material on dry paper.

PROJECT

A TRIPTYCH OF THOUGHTS

This project is aimed at combining many of the techniques we have been using and discussing in this chapter. You will need the full studio set up and equipment used thus far in this chapter, plus a minimum of three sheets of paper, ideally pre-soaked and damp, ready to print. This project is aimed at engaging with the imagination and we will not be using any objects or scenes from around us to inspire this, but we will be working purely from our heads.

Each print will be worked individually from the plastic matrix, cleaned or partially cleaned, between each new print. This process will mean that you will begin to gain a rhythm of spontaneous expression, as well as gaining some potential elements from the first print to re-use in the next. By the time the third is produced, there will inevitably be a sense of continuity in imagery and technique, but you will have loosened also in mark-making and expression.

The completed triptych will be complex and layered. But all of these have been created in a single pull. It is incredible what can be achieved with a little imagination, playfulness and an attentiveness to the matrix surface.

Print 1

Cutting up Tetra Pak is always a good way to start creating.

Individual forms can have texture applied in a loose manner.

Build up the image on the plastic, using masks and drawing.

The completed first matrix ready to print under the press.

The first impression of three which at this stage is tight.

Print 2

Removing previous card reveals textured backs to be printed.

Applying another layer of solid black on the plastic sheet.

Using a rag to remove bold, dynamic areas in the black ink.

Re-using the Tetra Pak: the backs and re-working the front.

Building the second image on the matrix with further drawing.

The third matrix ready, integrating fresh and re-used elements.

The second impression is building in complexity and interest.

Without cleaning, the second matrix is being re-used directly.

Print 3

A mask is being used to generate a strong shape for inking up.

Ink is being rolled up directly to partially ink the plastic.

More Tetra Pak elements are being created, added and re-used.

The third matrix ready to pull has numerous complex layers.

The final and third single pull print is alive and complex.

CHAPTER 4

EXPRESSIVE PAPER DRY-POINT

Paper dry-point is a highly versatile intaglio method of printmaking. The technique has gained recent momentum and interest amongst professional printmakers as the unique expressive potentials are fully explored. Due to the nature of the thin card that is used as the printing plate, it can easily be torn, cut, crumpled and manipulated in many ways that other intaglio print plates, such as a metal etching plate, may not. Apart from access to a printing press, no other specialist workshop set-up is required, which makes it very accessible for those new to intaglio printmaking. In this chapter we will explore paper dry-point and the mark-making options available, from traditional intaglio tools to integrating the techniques we have already explored. You will also see how we can use it to layer and build compositions that are fun, energetic and distinctive.

WHAT IS DRY-POINT?

Dry-point is a method of intaglio printmaking. Intaglio printmaking describes the process of creating drawn incised lines and marks upon the surface of a print matrix. Ink is forced into these marks and removed from all other areas of the plate that do not have incised marks. Therefore, the lines drawn are the lines that will print black. The first use of dry-point was on metal plates, often in combination with acid etched marks. Sharp tools are used to incise the surface of the metal, creating a burr either side of the line. No acid baths or acid etching are used, hence the term 'dry-point'.

To print the image, ink is spread across the plate to cover the marks and then gently removed by wiping away. During the wiping process, the ink is held within the incised lines and the burr that has been kicked up either side of each line.

Drawing with a mini grater onto dry-point card.

When the plate is then gently wiped clean, the surface ink is removed, whilst the incised dry-point marks hold onto ink. The plate is printed underneath a high pressure etching press onto damp paper. This method of inking and printing is very similar across all forms of intaglio printmaking, including etching. A dry-point print often has a characteristic faint ink haze, or softness, around each printed mark. This is because of the small amount of ink that becomes difficult to fully wipe clean next to the burr of the dry-point line. Nowadays, dry-point is also created upon acrylic sheets and of course there is paper dry-point.

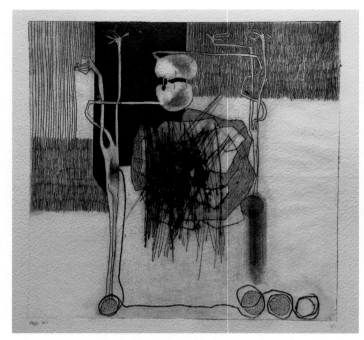

Stump People, Mary Dalton. This paper dry-point was printed under a heavy cast-iron press and the detail picked up is phenomenal. The range of marks shows how paper dry-point is capable of a huge amount of textural information.

Dry-point artists will also use other dry tools, such as sandpaper, dremels, graters, files and many more to create expressive marks and tonal value. Anything that scratches the surface of the printmaking matrix has the potential to create an impression.

PAPER DRY-POINT

Paper dry-point is a relatively new intervention within the printmaking world. It has been used for many years as a means for print educators to teach children intaglio printmaking without the chemical hazards or costs associated with metal etching. However, professional artists are now realizing that the marks and versatility of the method have huge potential to create complex and expressive prints.

The print matrix is a flexible piece of grey card (approximately 0.5 mm thick) with one side white and covered in a very thin layer of clear plastic. In essence, it is very similar to commercial plastic-coated card used for long-life milk, fruit juices or plant milks. The card is so thin it easily cuts with everyday scissors and can be torn, scrunched and folded with no strain. The artist can also purchase the card in large sheets at a very reasonable cost, allowing for large-scale expressive print works.

How Does it Work?

The plastic coating on the card replaces the metal or acrylic sheet. Tools are used to incise the plastic surface, either penetrating

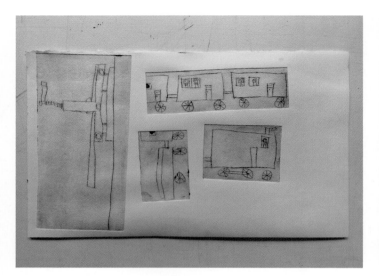

Paper Train, Guiwenneth Street, aged seven. Paper dry-point is a fantastic medium for children as well as professional artists.

the plastic to reveal the grey card below or just gently scratching the top layer. Due to the nature of the plastic coating, when the plate is inked up using the intaglio method the ink will wipe off smoothly, remaining only in the marks made. This sounds very logical and conventional. What makes paper dry-point unusual mainly hinges upon two things: firstly, you can use blunt tools and everyday objects to make marks; secondly, you can easily cut up the card. Both these factors are crucial to making paper dry-point very accessible and dynamic. The types of tools available to the artist can range from crochet hooks to garden twine, rather than having to stick with specific traditional dry-point tools. The print matrix can be torn or cut up into any desired shape and used like collage, layering individual elements before printing. Suddenly printmaking becomes very expressive, fluid and alive.

Materials

- Paper dry-point card or Tetra Pak
  The paper dry-point card can be purchased in sheets of various sizes and can be cut with scissors or a craft knife to the appropriate size. When cutting down the card, note carefully if there is a small strip along one side that has no plastic coating. You should be able to ascertain this by holding the card to the light and the strip will not be glossy. This strip needs to be cut off, as it inks up completely differently from the plastic-coated area and appears extremely unsightly.

  Tetra Pak produces marks very similar to the dry-point card. However, you have to work around the dimensions of the flat packed packaging. You will also need to clean the packaging before use. You are able to use the inside to avoid the printed information on the outside detracting from your

Printmaking specific paper, dry-point card is similar in nature to commercial Tetra Pak.

A good selection of mark-making tools can range from household objects to intaglio tools.

mark-making, but it does produce a slightly different mark. Testing would be advisable. If you can work with both of these issues, then it is very economical and accessible, as well as re-using an otherwise waste product. If you choose to use it for the projects in this chapter, please make appropriate decisions on its sizing in relation to the project set so that you are able to continue.

- Mark-making tools, such as:
  - An etching needle or dressmaker's sewing needle embedded into a cork, sharp end out.
  - A knitting needle of any size
  - A range of sandpaper scraps
  - A selection of household objects that have a sharp surface, such as a cheese or nutmeg grater, a citrus zester, a dressmaking rotary marker, a screwdriver.
- A few samples of textured surfaces that are flat and able to go safely under the press, for example, lace, wool, twine, netting. (Metal objects or stiff organic twigs are unable to go under the press; think of sacking hessian as your thickest material.)
- Scissors
- Craft knife and cutting mat
- Printing press set to intaglio pressure (*see* Chapter 10)
  An etching press is required for printing paper dry-point. Any etching press will work, ranging from tabletop varieties to cast-iron floor standing presses. If you are able to access a high-quality cast-iron press with a large bottom roller, then you will notice the difference in print quality. There are many open-access printmaking studios in the country with such presses; details are at the back of the book. The set-up of the press will be covered later in this chapter.

A small table-top etching press is great for producing little dry-points.

- Ink (black and a small colour selection)
- Old plastic credit/loyalty card
- Palette knife
- Paper (minimum weight 120 gms, smooth surface)
- Water spray bottle and water

- Clean sponge
- Old cotton rags (three or four, approximately 40cm square)
- Protective clothing for body and hands
- Clean-up materials
- Workspace (an ink-free area to draw and an area to ink up the plate with a suitable protective surface or a wipe down glass/plastic top – it gets very inky).

PROJECT

HAVING FUN WITH THE FIRST DRY-POINT

Paper dry-point marks can range from ephemeral to gestural. It all depends on what tool you are using and how much pressure you apply. To begin with, have fun exploring and embracing all the tools at your disposal. Any tool with a point ranging from the sharpness of a sewing needle to the bluntness of a 10mm knitting needle will create a line. Coarse sandpaper will create a completely different effect from fine wire wool; a nail hit into the surface of the card will create some pleasing, if loud, marks. The possibilities are endless and so to completely explore the freedom of this process from mark-making, to inking through to printing, we shall dive straight in and create a test print from a single sheet of dry-point card. This project is not one to plan an image for, or refer to imagery, sketchbook or still life, but one to allow you to be completely expressive with the tools you have around you. What tool was used, how it was applied and how it printed can all be documented along the way in note form on paper or even through photography/film. In this exercise we must encourage complete and utter free expression with the tools, not to become hindered by their technical aspect, but to embrace the expressive qualities and to engage with the card with dynamic energy.

Set-Up

For this project you will need a piece of dry-point card approximately 30 × 30cm. If working with packaging, I would suggest you use the full packaging net, cleaned, dried and laid flat without cutting up. You will also need a full range of tools to use, following the materials list earlier as guidance. Please make sure you have the full printmaking equipment list and workspace set up ready to go, and you have paper cut to size to fit the card plus borders.

Raven, Anna Fenton. An artist's dry-point produced on her first paper dry-point course illustrating a wonderful array of mark-making and energy. This was produced with a background matrix and a raven matrix, inked differently and printed together in a single pull.

Creating Marks: Line, Texture, Tone

The tools used on the card must make an impression on the surface of the plastic coating. For instance, sanding the plastic will scuff up the surface and create a printed impression. Scratching a line in the surface all the way through to the grey card will also create a printed impression. If you make holes in the card it does not matter. In fact, they can also print rather beautifully. The important thing to remember when using your tools is that the harder you press with your tool, the darker the printed impression will be. The dry-point card is pressure sensitive, so bear this in mind when drawing. In this exercise we are not wanting to think too much about an image, but more a collection of marks made with the various tools with the complete and utter abandonment of a child exploring. If you are really enjoying the mark-making of a particular tool, note it down on a piece of paper. Remember, though, that the printed impression will be in reverse, so make sure to note this. Or you can take a photograph or a video of the tool in action as a reminder. Try to let it not hinder your enjoyment of the tool

An etching needle is a great place to start creating marks.

Sandpaper of different grades scuffs the top plastic surface.

Try out different household items to make more unusual marks.

The alternative tools often make marks you are not expecting.

A craft knife can be used to peel away the plastic coating.

Use a craft knife to make holes for a more graphic quality.

itself, as we too often get distracted from being attentive to the task in hand. To understand what marks you have made, you can feel the card for the depth of the line with a nail, or hold it up to the light to see if you have scuffed the surface at all. This becomes quite tactile and allows you to engage further with the surface of the card.

Inking

When applying and wiping the ink onto your plate, it is so critical to not get despondent over how long it is taking to wipe the surface ink off. It is also critical to wear gloves if you do not like ink on your hands. It will get very inky. Follow the gentle circular motions described and soon you will see your marks emerge from the darkness. Rushing at this stage – scrubbing, attempting to polish your plate – will result in over-wiping. This means that too much ink has been removed in the wiping stage so that when

it comes to printing, the marks do not print at all.

You will never get the dry-point card back to its glossy white. There will always be a residual ink stain on the background of the card, called the plate tone. Often this will not print, and if it does it will be a very subtle grey and will not detract from the image. More complex and expressive wiping techniques to utilize the plate tone and other effects will be covered later in this chapter.

As you get further along the path of paper dry-point, assessing your marks before inking becomes second nature. It should not be daunting, and certainly is not difficult. It requires a sensitivity to the surface and a little patience. In this project we are following a basic inking and wiping technique, and you may notice as you wipe down, that some of the ink in the shallow marks – made with a knitting needle or similar soft-tipped item – skids out and leaves no ink. If the dry-point impression in the plastic

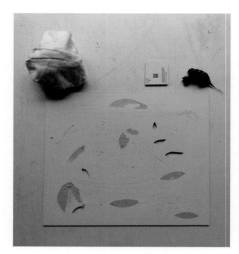

The materials needed for inking up the paper dry-point card.

Using the scraper, drag the ink out across the card's surface.

Drag the ink out in all directions until the card is covered.

Using a neat ball of cotton rag, carefully wipe down the ink.

Continue wiping in circular motions until marks are revealed.

The last wipes should be light and quick in circular motions.

The plate is ready to print when the marks are clear and even.

has no sharp edge, then the ink risks being wiped cleanly out of the mark since there is no burr or deep impression keeping the ink in the plastic. To avoid this, take a soft wrist action and very gentle caress when using the cloth to wipe ink off. Additionally, try using an inky rag to wipe down first, rather than a clean rag. The clean rag can be too aggressive to start with and remove a large amount of ink too quickly. Pay attention at each wiping stage and if you feel you are beginning to wipe too much away, stop. It is very easy to over-wipe delicate marks and thus remove all ink information. If your delicate, soft mark is surrounded by stronger marks, then you can always proceed with a general wipe down of the whole plate, and then use a small pad of cloth to specifically wipe the stronger marks down further, avoiding the delicate ones.

Some printmakers will polish the surface of the plate with a piece of clean tissue paper or even newsprint. This technique can help remove tiny residual ink at the edges of the marks in the dry-point card, thus creating a crisper final print. Whether to proceed with this final polish depends on your plate; if you have a lot of deeply incised sandpaper, scratch, needle marks or similar, then the final polish will print them cleaner. If, however, you have softer tonal marks or lines made with blunt-tipped objects, then the polish can risk removing the delicate layer of ink already present, a similar problem to over-wiping. After assessing the plate, if you wish to give it a polish, then using a small piece of tissue paper, approximately the size of your hand, lay it flat on the dry-point surface and using the heel of your hand, very gently, move the tissue around the inked surface in small circles using the pressure of your hand to keep the tissue in place and polishing the surface.

The edges and the back of the card gather ink. It is important to check that there are no large blobs of ink on the underside or at the edge prior to printing. These can print or get squeezed out under the press, causing a very dark smear. If you wish to create a very clean edge to the print, after inking you can trim off the very smallest edge using a ruler and a knife. It will remove the inky edge of exposed grey card. You cannot really clean this edge off, since the grey board has absorbed the black ink, so trimming is the best option. It does, however, cause the plate to subsequently get smaller and smaller, so is not appropriate for editioning.

Check the edges and underside of the card for ink blobs before printing.

Printing

When printing paper dry-point I would advise you to print onto damp paper. The ink is sitting in the incised lines and if we print onto damp paper, the paper fibres are slightly relaxed, allowing them to be forced more easily into these lines under the press, thus picking up more detail and subtle effects. There are various ways to dampen paper, but for this first project where I wish to encourage a joy of the marks and spontaneity, I would advise damping your dry paper directly with a spray bottle or wet sponge immediately before printing. Before handling the paper, clean your hands, remove inky gloves, or use little paper fingers to hold the clean paper. Paper fingers are small rectangles of clean stiff paper folded in half that you use as grips to hold paper, preventing ink transfer from your fingers.

To dampen the paper, if using a spray bottle, hold the paper at arm's length from the nozzle and apply a fine mist of water, front and back. Place the paper in between two sheets of newspaper or blotting paper and pat down to remove any excess water puddles. You are ready to print. If using a wet sponge, make sure that the sponge is not dripping, but you have gently squeezed out any excess water. When ready to print, lay the printing paper down on a clean surface and apply the wet sponge in broad flat strokes across the paper, one time for each stroke. This only needs to be done on the printing side of the paper. You are now ready to print. In Chapter 10, I have gone over a full pre-soaking routine for paper, but this spray/sponge method is a quick and effective method for test prints.

When laying your plate down onto the press bed to print, place a piece of tissue paper down first. This protects the press bed from the ink gathered on the back of your dry-point card. It is advisable to have your plate ready to print on the press bed before preparing paper so that you are ready to print as soon as your paper is dampened.

If you wish to print your plate again, then to get a clean impression, you will need to re-ink and wipe again and then print. If you print without re-inking, the image will be paler. This is called the ghost print, and will be discussed later.

BEYOND THE FIRST MARKS

The first dry-point marks are always such a joy to behold. They jump off the page and it can take you hours to understand their complexities in texture and expression. It is now we can look at both the printing plate and the printed image to understand and explore more deeply the techniques involved, but crucially without losing any of that gusto found in the first project.

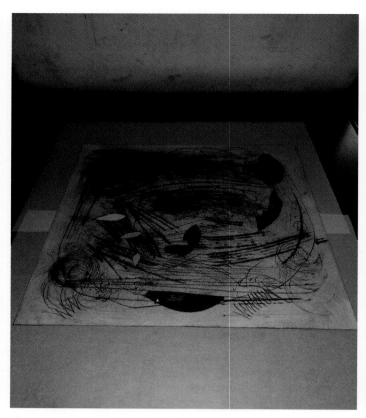

Place the matrix on the press bed on top of clean tissue paper.

Place your damp paper over the matrix and pull blankets down.

Once run through the press, the paper is gently peeled away.

The completed test print illustrating a full range of marks.

Pressure

The dry-point card is pressure sensitive. You will have noticed that if you had made some affirmative and heavy marks on your test plate, they will have printed more richly than the more feathery marks. The heavier you apply pressure with your tool into the card's surface, the more ink it will hold, thus the darker the printed line. This can be used to your advantage when wishing to express different elements of a work. Below are three examples of marks made with the same tool, applying heavy pressure through to lighter pressure on the right. It is clear to see how the marks could be used for a range of tonal values and expression in a print.

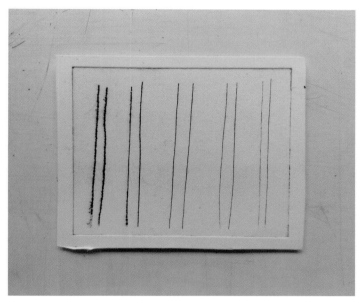

Etching needle lines decreasing in pressure, left to right.

Sandpaper marks decreasing in pressure, left to right.

Embossing

Embossing means pressing a textural surface into another surface to create a non-inked impression. Paper dry-point is very sensitive to pressure and works beautifully as the receiving surface for embossing. The resultant imprint into the dry-point card will hold ink during wipe down and therefore print as a replica of the texture embossed. It works best to emboss the dry-point surface under the printing press to achieve a deep imprint, although some very subtle results can be created by hand pressure.

When selecting materials for embossing, it is crucial that no metal objects (for instance metal mesh or wire) go under the press. It will damage your blankets and potentially the press itself. Likewise, select fabrics and other materials sensibly, not forcing twigs or thick fabrics under the press. A general rule of thumb is not to go beyond thick hessian sacking if embossing under the press. It is also advisable to use some old blankets in the press, or even just a couple of layers of newsprint, to replace your printing blankets. This is to prevent any high pressure transferring the emboss into the felt blankets, which will subsequently affect your and others' intaglio prints.

When inking any area of embossing, be gentle and patient when wiping down, as it easily skids out of the marks, particularly if you have embossed soft items such as textiles or organic materials. It is often prudent to leave a touch more ink on the surface rather than attempting to wipe your plate clean.

After printing embossed surfaces, the subtle imprint in the card gets compressed under the pressure of the printing press and thus holds less ink in subsequent inking and it does not edition very well. If, however, you are exploring unique prints, then embossing is a strong expressive mark that can produce beautiful results, especially when combined with other, bolder marks.

A small collection of a range of suitable embossing materials.

Preparing to emboss some hessian and elastic bands under the press.

The embossed dry-point is very delicate and requires careful wiping to print.

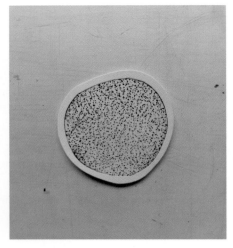

Sandpaper is a stronger emboss and creates a beautiful effect when printed.

PROJECT

CUTTING IT ALL UP

Paper dry-point is extremely versatile and expressive, even if the most basic of mark-making tools are used. We have seen that different pressures, the toolkit and your inking technique can all dramatically alter the printed outcome. One of the most unique aspects of paper dry-point is its ability to be able to be cut up easily. Try it yourself. Make sure you have noted down any marks you find interesting from the tester prints in the previous project, or even photographed the plate. You can gently wipe the plate of excess ink with a clean rag before cutting. Then, take a pair of hand scissors and start cutting it up, or even tearing it. Try making holes in it with a scalpel, hole punch or big nail.

Turn your card into about five or six different elements. Note that when you tear the card, if you tear one way you end up with the exposed grey card on the printing side. If you tear the other way this exposed card is on the underside. As we have seen previously, any areas of exposed grey card will ink up very dark, so utilize this jagged torn grey edge to your advantage for bold, unpredictable edges.

Once you have your pieces, ink them all as individual pieces. Be careful inking up around any holes or around very small pieces. Sometimes it helps if you wipe down the smaller pieces in the palm of your hand.

They can now be printed in any free arrangement. You can overlap pieces up to three layers before the press struggles with the increase in depth and thus pressure. If you do choose to overlap, you will end up with an emboss of the underneath card on the top layers and this may ink up on the next print. This is something to be broadly aware of, but not something to stop the wonderful collage potentials of the card.

This method of printing dry-point card allows for a huge amount of creativity on the press bed, arranging pieces directly and in a free-form approach. There are very few printmaking methods, particularly within intaglio, that allow for such direct ease in cutting up unusual shapes. It also allows you to ink each piece separately, creating a unique effect on each one.

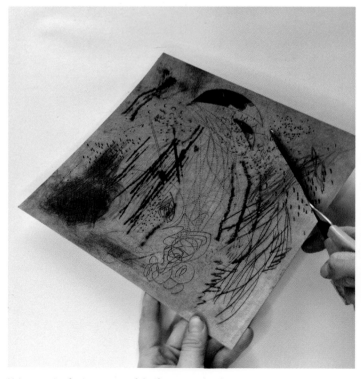

Using a pair of scissors or craft knife, cut up the dry-point.

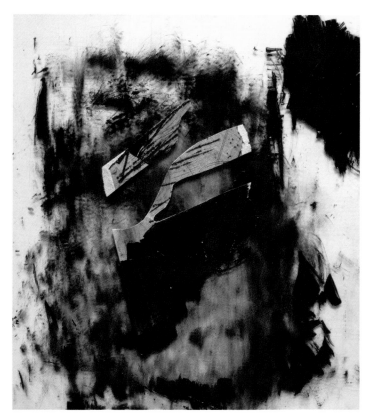

Ink up each section individually, allowing for varying effects.

Arrange the inked sections on the press bed, overlapping some.

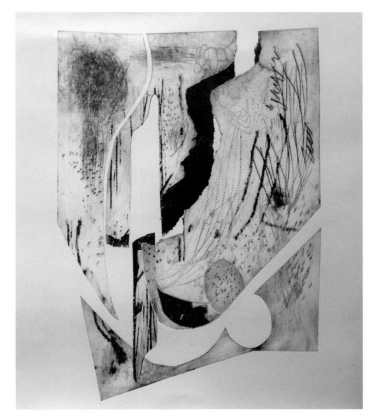

The completed cut up dry-point has a similarity to a collage.

A student pulling a large format cut up dry-point from the press.

ALTERNATIVE TECHNIQUES

We are now going to look at how we can exploit the expression and versatility of dry-point even further by integrating some other printmaking techniques onto our dry-point plate.

Stamping and Monoprint

The most useful material element of the dry-point card is the fact that it has a wipe-down plastic coating. This plastic coating can be used as a surface for monoprint, which we have looked at in previous chapters and ink can be applied directly to the card after the intaglio inking has been completed. In addition, you can stamp relief marks onto the plastic surface using some of the relief forms from Chapter 2. When printed, both the intaglio marks and the direct ink marks will form the image. These techniques are extremely interchangeable and can be mixed at will upon the surface of the dry-point card.

When introducing non-intaglio effects to the card, it is vital that this is done after all the intaglio dry-point lines have been inked and wiped to the artist's satisfaction. After the addition of monoprint or relief textures onto the surface, then the intaglio marks cannot be wiped down since you would smudge all your newly added ink.

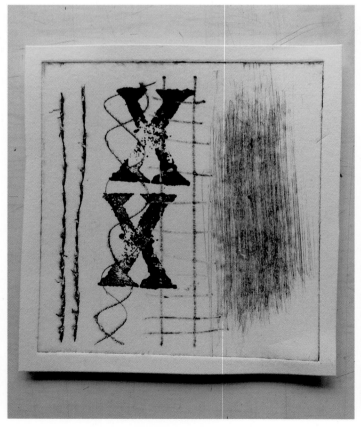

Stamping directly on inked card prior to printing produces bold results.

Innovative Wiping Techniques

Wiping down the dry-point plate does not have to be all elbow grease and sweat. In fact, the wiping technique is extremely dynamic and a great way to introduce energy to an otherwise static print.

Wiping techniques explored through numerous fun test pieces are near endless. I have broken down the main ones through small examples, each created on a piece of dry-point card that has the same marks on, made using an etching needle, a knitting needle and some coarse sandpaper.

Wiping can really change the atmosphere of a work. I have created two dry-point images of a basic candle and window. Both were inked up: the first was wiped down cleanly; in the

A cleanly wiped card and the resultant impression is predictable.

Using different wiping techniques, a similar image has life and soul.

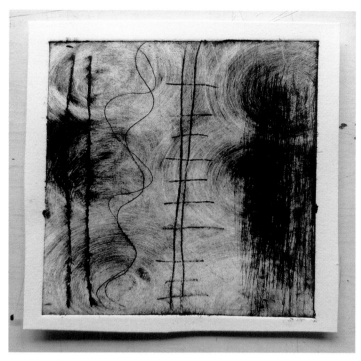

The print after leaving the circular rag marks on the card.

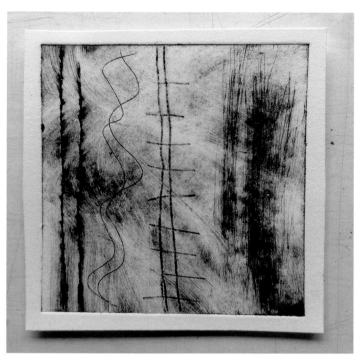

The print after creating a random wipe tone on the card.

Plate tone was removed in the middle third to create delicate tonal change in the print.

A rag was used to remove some monoprint stamping prior to printing.

second I used some wiping techniques to give the image more life and atmosphere. The difference is clear and illustrates the importance of wiping as a means of artistic impression.

Scrunching

The dry-point card is very easy to tear and scrunch up. The crinkles created through the scrunching process hold ink beautifully and produce a very unusual impression. The torn edges of the card will hold slightly more ink and print a lovely mottled dark grey through to black, depending on how vigorously you wipe down. The card can be scrunched at random or even specifically folded.

The Ghost

We have come across ghost printing in previous chapters. The ghost describes any print that is pulled from the plate after the first impression, without re-inking. It will inevitably be paler, hence the name 'ghost'. The ghost in dry-point is highly effective and if you have strong lines or heavy inking which holds much ink, then the ghost print can continue to be printed for many impressions, each one getting subsequently paler. This can be used to your advantage to create depth within the image. If you are wishing to play with the first impression and the ghost within the same print, then you can use thin paper masks to prevent ink being transferred to your paper as you run it through the press. These masks can then be removed after the first impression, the print run through again and the masked areas will print as the ghost onto your paper.

If using a multiple run through technique, then you can 'trap' your paper in the rollers of the press bed. This means you do not run the paper off out of the rollers, but keep it trapped between and gently lift it off the dry-point plate so that it remains in the same position in relation to the plate on the press bed. You can then add/remove further masks and print again. When using this technique, the paper that originally was dampened will be gradually drying as you print multiple runs. This means that it will also be shrinking and so you may get a misalignment of your dry-point marks as they run through the press again. This means you need to act quickly and limit the number of times through the press to three or four. You can sponge the paper lightly again before it is printed or even place a piece of clean plastic over the paper to prevent water evaporation whilst you are preparing to print.

COLOUR

As we have seen, paper dry-point is highly successful when used in a monochrome effect. It can also be inked up with colour. The inking and wiping process is exactly the same, but it is worth noting that the strength of the marks will be visually weaker because there is less contrast between the colour line work and the white paper. The darker inks work well to showcase the very

Scrunching up the card creates a beautiful impression.

A dry-point inked up ready to print with tissue paper protecting the top.

The first pull off the press with the paper remaining trapped in the rollers.

The print about to go under the press again with a further tissue mask placed on.

The completed print with first impression at the bottom, and two ghost impressions.

fine work such as embossing, sanding or fine etching needle line, which is lost when you ink up in the paler or higher tones, such as yellow. If you are wishing to introduce colour line work, then I would advise to start with the two following methods and experiment with their potentials.

Inking up in Colour

Inking up in a single colour is exactly the same as inking up in black. The plate tone will be a residual haze of your ink colour. The darker colours can be read more easily than the high tones, such as yellow. Coloured inks can be used direct from the tube or mixed to requirements. Each colour should have its own wiping rag, as otherwise cross-colour contamination can happen when wiping down. If you wish to print a plate in blue and then the same plate in yellow, the initial blue ink will stain the subsequent yellow ink and turn it green. It is best to work from the paler colours, such as yellow, through to the darker ones, such as blue, if you are experimenting in this fashion. Or keep plates of different colours separate.

À La Poupée

This technique describes applying specific colours of ink to specific areas of the plate, wiping down and printing. The colours are kept separate on the plate and the edges blended when it

Tangential Threads, Nina Gross. A stunning example of a paper dry-point using both monochrome and colour. The pebbles have been individually cut, marked, and inked up in differing colours. The hand was created using monoprint techniques through a mask and the thread was printed using inked-up string under the press. The colour dry-point integrates perfectly with the other print techniques.

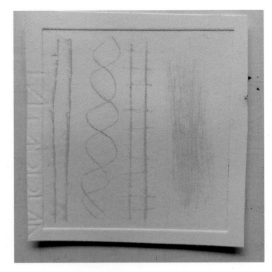

Yellow ink can lose some details from the finer marks.

comes to the wiping down stage. If for instance, you applied a yellow ink section and a blue ink section, when you wiped down and the two merged, there would be a green edge between the two. Each colour requires its own wipe down rag so as to not cross-contaminate colour too much beyond the edge. *À la poupée* works best when you are allowing the inks to be free and blend.

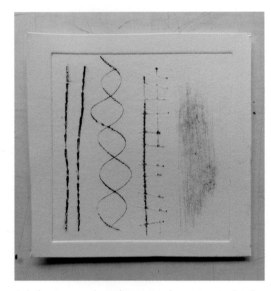

A darker tone, such as ultramarine, keeps true to details.

Use separate colours to carefully ink up the card matrix.

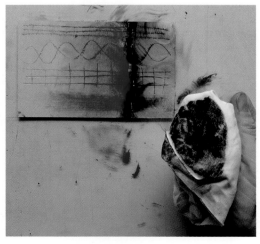

Use different rags for each colour to wipe down the inks.

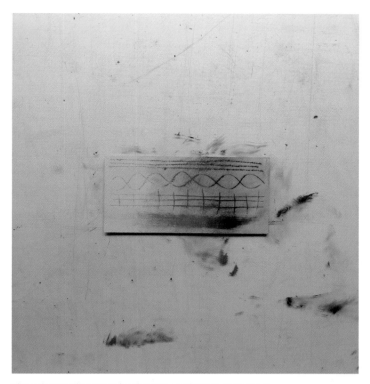

The colours will gently blend on the card where they meet.

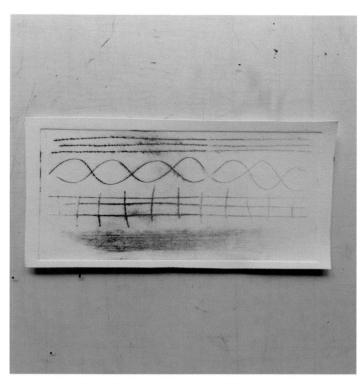

The *à la poupée* impression has a beautiful, blended effect.

Roll-Over

A very effective way of introducing colour to a dry-point plate is to use a roll-over technique. This involves applying a thin layer of colour over the top of an inked up dry-point plate, thus providing a general all over background colour to the print. This roll-over technique can be used even if the stamping technique has been used on the card. The colour chosen for the roll-over has to be a different viscosity, or oiliness, from the ink used to ink up the dry-point plate, the reason being that the change in viscosity of the roll-over ink prevents the roller from picking up the stiffer ink used on the dry-point card, which would contaminate the roll-over ink. This type of colour work is described as

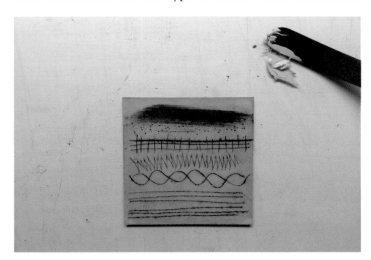

Mix a loose ink ready to roll over your inked dry-point card.

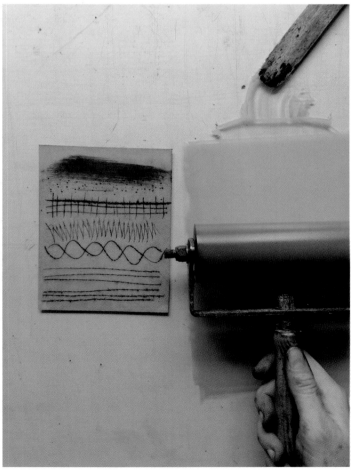

Roll out a very thin layer of ink using a hard rubber roller.

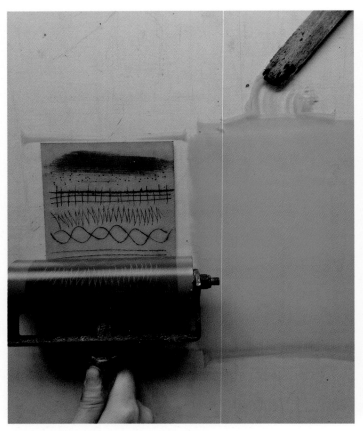

Roll over the card in one motion, with no reversing of the roller.

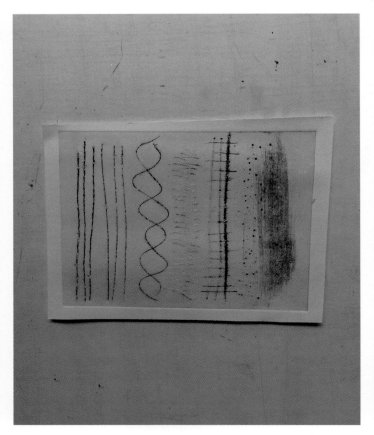

The completed impression has an all-over coloured background.

Duff Pile, Mary Dalton. This paper dry-point was inked up in a very dark purple and had an opaque pale pink roll-over applied. The result is simple and effective.

viscosity printing. To change the viscosity, add approximately two drops of linseed oil to a 50p size amount of your roll-over ink. You should see the change in ink texture, from stiff and tacky to looser and glossier.

COMBINING IT ALL

When working expressively with paper dry-point, it is already clear that the possibilities are numerous and indeed so flexible that it will suit many languages of expression. In order to avoid getting overwhelmed when wanting to create a composed work, create a 'toolkit' of techniques that suit your personal style and desired result. In essence, try many techniques with numerous tools and find the ones that suit your particular needs. Once you have found the tools and marks you like, then you can really develop their individual expression within your work.

Dry-point works very successfully when areas of the print are also allowed to breathe, where they do not have any marks on them. Numerous marks are extremely expressive in dry-point, but can overwhelm an image, so think carefully before making those incisions in the surface. Since the marks cannot be erased from the dry-point surface, it sometimes is worth taking your time to consider which mark to make and then act decisively. If you can balance these marks with bold areas of negative space, where there is no information, then it can really bring the print alive.

PROJECT

DYNAMIC STILL LIFE

This project is designed as a follow along; use the guidance to allow for your own interpretation of the subject matter. It is a project that will enable you to put many of the ideas into practice, combining the alternative print methods with the more traditional intaglio techniques. You will need to choose a subject matter as a focus for the mark-making, not as something to attempt to directly replicate. I wish to encourage the freedom of mark-making from earlier exercises and to be bold with more interpretive and abstract forms. I have chosen a pot plant, but the subject matter can be of your own choice.

Cutting directly into the card is a great, bold way to start.

Use a range of tools to change the weight of the drawn lines.

A good selection of still life objects serves as inspiration.

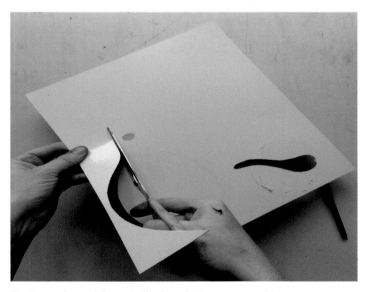

Cutting up the card dramatically alters the image composition.

Altering the pressure you use with tools keeps the work alive.

Peeling away plastic will add some darker areas in the print.

Layering up sections of card gives many composition options.

Individual bits of card can have different techniques applied.

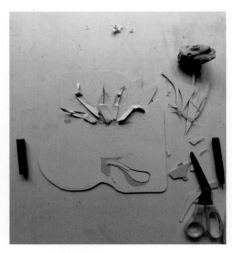

The finished composition, ready for inking and printing.

The work inked in black ready to receive further techniques.

Hand stamping is applied after inking and is a bold addition.

Colour roll-overs are applied as a final process to add zing.

The completed impression is bold and considered in choices.

COMPLEX HYBRID TECHNIQUES

Paper dry-point is a brilliant way to introduce very fine lines and details to more expressive prints. We have already looked at how we can generate some beautiful expressive marks in Chapter 2 and many of these approaches can be printed with a paper dry-point print. We can use multi-plate techniques to print complex impressions that combine multiple printing methods. Firstly, let us see how dry-point card only can be used as a multi-plate technique; secondly, we will look at the start of a hybrid print using dry-point and a monoprint plate.

Multi-Plate Printing

Multi-plate dry-point printing works very effectively and allows you to create independent printing matrices that can have completely separate marks and effects, but they all print one after each other on the same impression. This requires a very basic registration system to make sure all matrices are printing in the correct alignment with each other. Take a look at Chapter 10 on how to make a basic paper registration template. This is what we will be using. You will also need to make sure that the impression paper you use remains trapped in the roller, as with the ghost printing. We will take a look at the beautiful spiky pot plant used in the still life project to demonstrate how all this can be achieved.

Each card is inked in separate colours: yellow, dark green, black.

The cards can have ink applied with different techniques. Here we see some wipe marks left on the black matrix.

Three Tetra Pak cards cut to the same size and marks added.

Roll-overs can add another layer of interest to the matrices.

Lay down the yellow matrix upon a registration template. Add any masks if you so wish.

The first layer printed: cadmium yellow with a green viscosity roll-over. Note the impression paper and the template remain trapped under the rollers to ensure no movement of either.

Laying down the green matrix in position according to the guides on the registration template.

The second layer printed in register with the first.

Finally, the black, or key line, is added in register.

The completed three-plate paper dry-point print has a range of tones and a depth that could not be achieved in a single plate.

Multi-Plate Hybrid Printing

Using the pot plant example again, we will use the two-colour dry-point matrices from the previous demonstration and drop in a top layer of a monoprint, taking inspiration from Chapter 2. This begins to illustrate the potentials of unique and complex printmaking, where the layers and effects are used with conviction and energy to create a dynamic end impression. Printmaking is such fun!

The black monoprint created on a piece of plastic. A tissue paper mask has been added to mask off the non-image areas, leaving only the pot-plant silhouette exposed.

The completed pot plant using two paper dry-point plates in cadmium yellow and a dark green with a black monoprint third layer.

A detail of the pot plant illustrating the beautiful layering of the monoprint over the dry-point. The sense of energy and movement is very dynamic.

CHAPTER 5

MOKULITO

Mokulito, or wooden lithography, is possibly one of the most entertaining and wonderfully buoyant printmaking methods that is out there. It is absolutely wonderful. Furthermore, it can be hand printed or printed on a basic tabletop etching press, negating the need for specific lithography presses. Mokulito is worked upon a wooden matrix, enabling the artist to combine it with woodcut in the same print, and the grain of the wood can be manipulated to form part of the imagery. The lithographic marks work beautifully in combination with not just the woodcut carving, but also dry-point and monoprint. It is exciting, alive and a true printmaking gem. This chapter will cover the basic Mokulito on various different wood surfaces, from birch ply to solid maple. We will look at how to incorporate woodcut and various other print techniques to produce layered lithographic works.

LITHOGRAPHY: THE MAGIC EXPLAINED

So many times I have heard lithography referred to as magic. In the traditional lithographic methods, at a certain stage, the artist's image is removed from the matrix and thus visually only a faint ghost trace is left. A very greasy, non-drying black ink can then be rolled into the drawn image marks. The image then reappears on the matrix as the roll-up black ink replaces the previously removed drawn marks. It is certainly very magical to witness. What is actually happening is a very specific process based upon an understanding of both the matrix and the process involved in stabilizing the image upon the matrix surface. The stabilized image is printed with oil-based ink. The one crucial element that makes all of this possible, from stone litho through to Mokulito, is the understanding that oil and water do not mix.

Stone lithography is the first medium in the lithographic family tree, and these limestone slabs are what the artist draws on and prints from.

The artist will use grease-based drawing tools to generate their image on the surface of a specifically prepared lithographic matrix. These tools may be specialist lithographic materials or anything that may contain an element of grease, for instance vegetable oil, oil pastels, even your own finger. Once the drawing is complete, the matrix is coated with a thin layer of gum Arabic. Gum Arabic is a natural resin derived from the acacia tree.

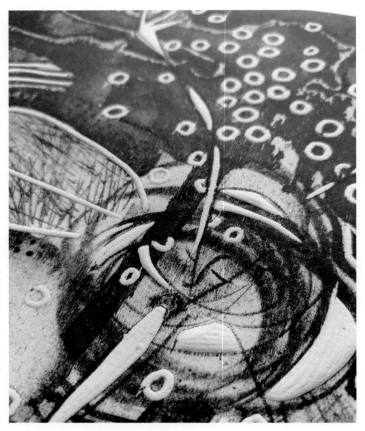
A detail of a Mokulito print shows the wonderful textures possible.

The gum is mildly acidic and reacts with the surface of the matrix, allowing the greasy drawn areas to stabilize and attract oil-based ink, and the non-image areas to remain damp and repel the oil-based ink. This is often referred to (confusingly) as 'etching' the matrix. Once complete, traditional lithography will have a second etch and the greasy image drawing will be replaced with a uniform layer of non-drying ink. Mokulito skips this stage. To print, the gum is washed off and the matrix kept damp with clean water and all is rolled up in oil-based ink. The drawing created with greasy tools will attract the oil-based ink, and the non-image areas which are being kept continuously damp will repel the oil-based ink. Thus, only the image receives ink and it can be printed, creating a direct positive impression of the artist's drawing.

Wooden Lithography

Wooden lithography was first experimented with and used in Japan in the 1970s. It has always been on the sidelines of print-making and is quite an elusive medium. There are a few artists who have been really pushing it into mainstream expression, and this is so valuable. Mokulito is not the best method if you wish to produce a high edition of the work. It is fickle and the plate will degrade after only a few prints, and it will reach a stage where the wooden grain of the matrix becomes more dominant than the drawing. However, if you are here to engage with print as a means of expression, rather than a means of editioning and business, then Mokulito is absolutely, unconditionally brilliant.

The wooden matrix used can vary hugely. The most common matrix is birch plywood, which in itself can come in a range of qualities and grains. Different woods will print differently. Some, such as birch ply, will have a strong wood grain that prints readily in the non-image areas, whilst others such as maple will have little grain printing in the background. Solid wood can also be used; however, most artists choose to use ply because it is cheaper, it is more readily available, and it does not buckle when it gets wet. However, the production of plywood and the formaldehyde glues involved are not great for the planet, so solid wood is better in this respect, especially if it can be sustainably sourced from well managed forests. Most Mokulito uses side-grain wood, such as ply, with the grain running across the matrix. However, I have been developing and looking into using end-grain wood in Mokulito. End-grain wood describes timber that is produced from a crosscut across the tree trunk, rather than a plank down the tree trunk (producing side grain). The theory is that the tighter grain of certain end-grain timber is a closer replication to the tight surfaces of lithographic stone or grained lithographic zinc sheets, thus producing a cleaner and more sensitive wooden matrix. This is still in its research phase, but it holds exciting potential.

End-grain timber is taken from a cross section across the trunk.

Printing

Due to the nature of the plywood matrix, the lithographic marks on the matrix can be printed with minimal pressure by hand or under an etching press, as long as you use runners to raise your roller (*see* Chapter 10 on how to insert runners). The Mokulito can also be treated as a woodcut and this can therefore be hand printed. A lot of Mokulito is printed with sponge-based rollers, like the rollers you would apply paint to a wall with. These rollers are attempting to replicate a traditional lithographic nap roller, which is made from the nap side of leather, producing a soft surface allowing the ink to be forced into the grease drawing. However, to re-use the foam rollers (if you do not wish to use solvent to clean them) you have to keep covering them with cling film or a similar product, as well as having to purchase a new roller for each colour you wish to use. I prefer a more sustainable approach if possible and have achieved great results (with good lithographic rolling technique) with a re-usable, high quality printmaking rubber roller.

Mokulito responds well to printing on damp paper to aid the pick-up of the more detailed marks. It will also print very well on dry paper. It is a case of assessing the matrix you have and making a decision based upon this. If printing by hand, it would be advisable to avoid using the heavy weight printing papers as the pressure required to get a decent impression on these would be too much by hand. Thus, a Japanese paper of around 40–80 gms would be perfect to allow a good impression to be made. This would not need dampening.

Materials

For the following chapter, the projects require some specialist lithographic drawing tools. These may seem rather costly at first, but they are essential for the lithographic process, and many of them will last you for years, so end up being very economical. Some communal studios who offer lithography may supply these materials to use or purchase in smaller quantities. Or you could team up with some friends and then divide the spoils! Do not be intimidated by the list of materials needed; I have explained each one and just work your way through it.

- Plywood
  To start with, we will be working on basic birch ply. This comes in various depths and you can get various grades. I would advise that you purchase some ply that is under 10mm in depth, nearer to 8mm. If you are printing on a press, you will need runners of the same depth. Make sure you get the best and smoothest ply you can, with the least number of imperfections. You can get this from a DIY store, or you can order artists' ply from many art retailers. You will need a couple of A4 sheets or the equivalent. Remember, sometimes it is cheaper to buy a larger sheet and cut it down to size if space permits.

  There will also be some work done on solid timbers, which are significantly more expensive. This is to show the effects that different woods have on the impression. It is not necessary to purchase these now, as you can follow along to understand the differences and purchase later.

A student pulling their very first Mokulito print.

Mokulito can use a range of different timbers.

- Gum Arabic

  This is essential for Mokulito. You can purchase gum Arabic in crystal form, which allows you to make up your own batches given time and preparation, or in pre-made solution form. For the ease of learning in this chapter, get the liquid gum so you need not have to make up your own. You can get natural and synthetic gum; I always recommend the natural gum if possible. If you buy the concentrated gum Arabic, then read the instructions to make sure you dilute it to the correct proportions. If you do a lot of lithography in the future, then it may be worth looking into purchasing the crystals to make up a specific batch of gum each time you require it. All of these can be bought from art/printmaking retailers.

- Lithographic drawing tools

  Although you can produce many lithographic marks without specific tools, for these projects it would be really useful to have a basic kit. This would include lithographic crayons ranging from hard to soft. You can get them in a box or individually. Different manufacturers label hard and soft crayons under different categorization systems, so please check before using. Lithographic drawing pencils are similar to the crayons but are shaped more like a traditional pencil and can be sharpened to a fine point. They are extremely useful, and some require a clutch pencil holder so please do check. Stick tusche will allow you to create wash effects. The stick tusche is less harmful to your health than the liquid tusche, and so I prefer to use it. A rubbing tablet (also known as an ink tablet) is a wonderful lithographic drawing tool that can create tonal effects through subtle smudging. Very useful and worth the investment. Finally, some drawing ink. This enables you to use a paintbrush or dip pen to create bold, expressive marks.

- Sandpaper

  Basic fine grade household sandpaper is perfect. It is important it is fine, or extra fine, as you do not want to scratch the wooden surface with a coarse sandpaper. A fine grade wire wool is also useful, but not essential.

- Oil-based ink

  It is essential that your ink is oil-based. The water-based inks will not work. We will be using black and some basic colours in the projects.

- Roller

  You will need a printmaking roller for Mokulito. Ideally, the roller width should be wider than the shortest side of your wooden matrix. This is the ideal. Do not worry if you do not have access to one this wide currently, as we can explore rolling technique to negate any problems.

- Paper

  You will need to have available some basic printing paper with as smooth a surface as possible. If you are hand printing, it is better to use a lightweight paper: Japanese paper under 80 gms is brilliant, and you can just use some print-out paper as testers. If printing under a press, you can use a heavier printing paper that you can dampen.

- Water, bucket and sponge

  You will need access to a water supply (I use rainwater to save tap water), a clean bucket to hold the water and several sponges. You can buy litho sponges, which are brilliant, but you can also use household sponges. They just need to be of a decent size to fit flat in your hand and have a sponge surface, not a scouring one.

- Brush

  A wide, soft bristled decorator's brush is ideal to apply the gum layer to your plate.

- French chalk or talc

  This is useful, but not essential. If using talc, make sure it is unscented and the simplest form.

- Woodcut tools

  Basic sets can be acquired cost effectively. The set should cover all you need for this chapter. Some lino tools can also double up as woodcut tools. Please check the manufacturer's guidance.

- Printing press or printing barren

  Your press needs to be able to raise its rollers to take the plywood. If hand printing, I advise a good wooden spoon or tough printing barren.

A selection of traditional lithographic drawing tools.

This project is just that: making sure you feel confident in making Mokulito print. It will also give you a great introduction into the basic principles of lithography. You will need all the drawing materials and a piece of A4 plywood ready to go. If working on scraps of ply, do not worry if it is an odd shape: just make sure you have enough surface area to be expressive with the tools, and make sure any rough edges are sanded smooth. The drawing and etching happen in the first instance, then the plate will need to sit for a few days before you ink. It all just builds the anticipation!

Preparing the Plate

To prepare the plywood, you will need to give it a quick sand. This will help remove any really heavy grain, splinters or rough areas, all of which can adversely affect your print. This is particularly important if using very basic ply, as the grain and surface can be rough. Please do take suitable precautions when sanding, such as wearing a face mask and working in a ventilated area. Try not to blow the sawdust off the ply, as this will make it go everywhere, just a light brush off outside is all it needs. You can

Using a fine grade wire wool to sand the matrix in the grain direction.

use your hands to hold the sandpaper flat, or a sanding block. Sand the ply following the grain, up and down, until the surface feels smoother to touch. It only needs a couple of passes. If using the wire wool, you can now sand it further. Be careful when removing the wire wool dust off the ply so as to not get any steel fibres near yourself or equipment.

Drawing

Once your plate is fully prepared, it is time to start the fun: drawing. When it comes to drawing on wood, you have to be aware that there is a grain to the wood, and this, particularly with washes, will influence your mark. It is part of the beauty of Mokulito. The litho tools are all grease-based, so you can also use any household item that also contains an element of grease – soap, vegetable oil, lipstick, butter. These items are to be experimented with freely; some will work, some will not.

This first project is about getting used to the effects and processes of the mark-making tools. So go ahead and draw on the surface of the plywood. Have a go with the solid tools first, such as the crayons and rubbing sticks. Generally speaking, the greasier the drawing crayon or pencil, the richer the black. The harder drawing tools, which contain less grease, are best for fine detail and shading. If your crayons are not labelled according to their grease content, then gently press your fingernail into the side and feel the resistance. The harder, less greasy tools feel significantly firmer than the greasier ones.

After the drawing tools, start to play with the ink, tusche and washes. Finally, have a go at a few alternative approaches or materials, such as hand stamping. Stick tusche requires dissolving in water to generate washes. To do this, scrape some dry stick on a clean surface, such as a ceramic plate, transferring a layer of grease. Then add a bit of water and massage with the tusche using a clean brush. It will eventually dissipate in the water. If you are wishing to use it at its full strength, it needs to look like Indian ink; otherwise, dilute as you wish. Note that if you build up layers of washes on the matrix, it may not actually print as you see. The washes may just 'fill in' with ink when rolled up because of the amount of grease laid down in layers onto the wooden surface. It is best to keep washes contrasting in their dilution, with not too many overlaid.

As you fill up the space, just be aware that you will need to leave areas for gestural mark-making with brushes, or larger areas of washes. There should be enough space for all; if not, just start a new ply matrix. Also be aware of noting down what marks were made where and with what tool. You can photograph as you go, make a written note or write in mirror writing on the actual matrix. It will be useful for further projects.

A soft litho drawing crayon tested at different pressures.

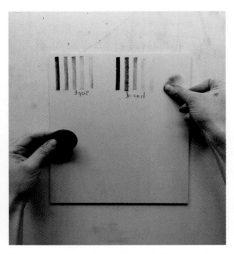

Use a finger to rub the tablet and then transfer the grease.

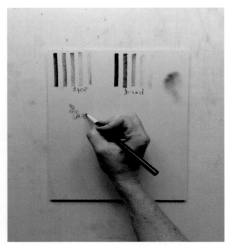

Using a soft litho drawing pencil to test a range of marks.

Using a rubbing lump within a mask generating a strong edge.

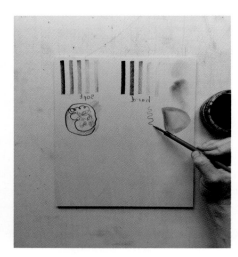

Using a dip pen and drawing ink to create fine, fluid lines.

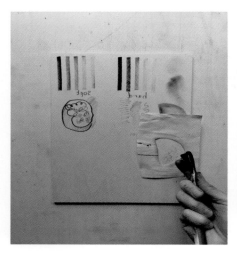

Using a mask to protect the matrix as ink splatters are made.

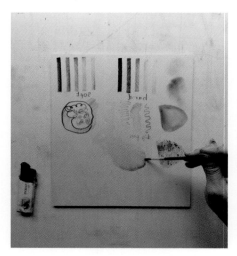

Adding drops of dissolved stick tusche into a water puddle.

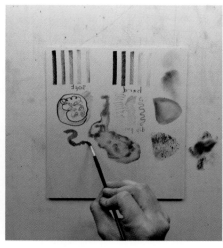

Using stick tusche to create washes of different strengths.

Bleeding drawing ink into a water puddle and leaving to dry.

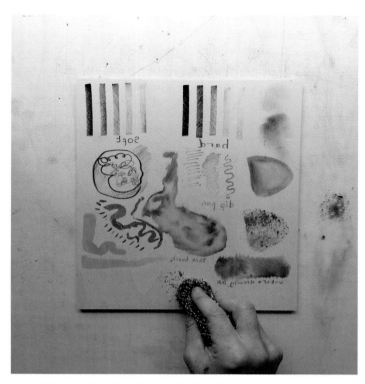

Using oil-based ink to stamp texture directly onto the wood.

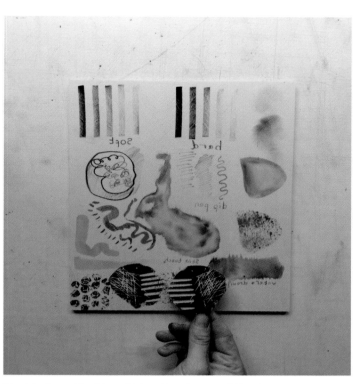

Lino inked up with oil-based ink and hand stamped directly.

Etching

Once your marks are complete, you will need to etch them to stabilize them on the matrix surface and to make sure the non-image areas repel the oil-based ink. This is done with gum Arabic. You will need to get the wide brush, French chalk (if using), a clean rag and the gum Arabic solution ready. Etching is a reasonably quick process, but after the gum has been applied the ply will need to sit for a minimum of 8 hours (e.g. overnight) or ideally a few days. This will help the etching process. If you can place the gummed matrix in sunlight, this will help with the reaction.

Printing

Here we go! Printing the Mokulito plate. It is always prudent with lithography to have everything available to hand, because it happens at speed and it cannot be left alone for too long when inking. If you neglect your matrix it can cause the plate to dry up, ink to fill in on non-image areas and many more problems. So make sure the workspace is set up with the black ink rolled up, the roller charged and ready, the press (if using) set to pressure and an inking space clear. You will need the bucket filled with a couple of inches of water, the sponge and your paper ready to print. If using a spray or sponge damping method, make sure

French chalk is sprinkled onto the surface of the dry matrix.

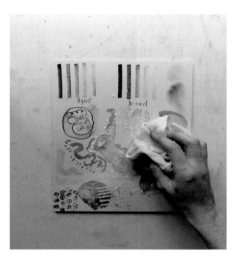

The chalk is gently patted out thinly using a clean muslin.

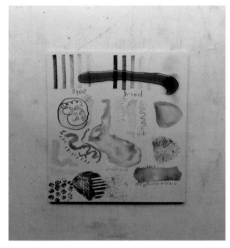

Gum Arabic is poured directly onto the surface of the matrix.

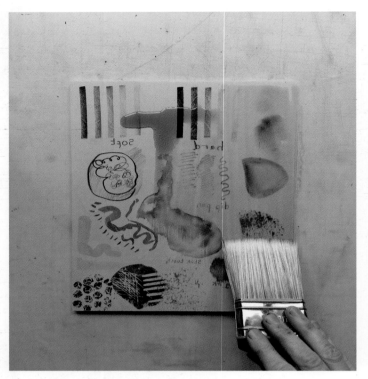

A clean, soft bristled brush is being used to spread the gum.

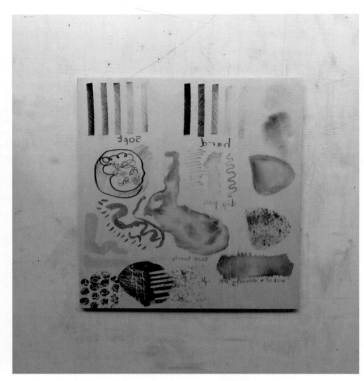

The completed matrix is safe under the gum Arabic etch layer.

this is ready to go. If hand printing, you will need to hand-print away from the inking area, so prepare a space ready.

In an ideal world, the width of your roller will be wider than one of the sides of your Mokulito plate. This prevents tram lines printing. Tram lines describe the edges of the printmaking roller leaving a set of parallel lines across your printing matrix. In Mokulito, this can occur and is easily negated by using a wider roller. If you have a narrower roller, then some quick rolling across a nice damp surface should 'whip' these lines away.

Inking lithographically is different from all the methods we have looked at so far. Do not panic if it does not work:

there is always more ply to start again, and it is crucial that you never give up or feel despondent if it does not ink well. Litho, and Mokulito in particular, are wonderfully stubborn and independent creatures, but they are also your friends through persistence and diligence. Take time, read and look over the instructions first, and have a go. Keep the plate damp at all times.

Hand-printing the plate follows the standard method we have already looked at. A fair amount of pressure will need to be applied because you are dealing with a very thin layer of ink on the matrix, so make sure that the paper is held firmly in place.

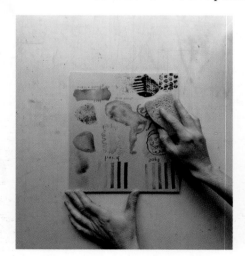

A clean sponge with clean water is used to wipe off the gum.

The plate is kept damp whilst rolled up using oil-based ink.

The plate is re-wiped with clean water to stay evenly damp.

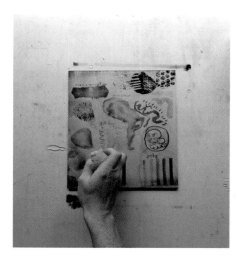

Some unwanted ink scumming is removed with squeezes of water.

The inked Mokulito plate is ready to print under the press.

Damp paper is placed on top of the Mokulito on the press bed.

An impression is gently pulled from the plate after printing.

The completed impression showcasing an array of litho marks.

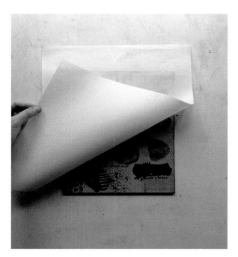

Place dry lightweight Japanese paper onto the inked surface.

Using a hand printing barren, apply even pressure all over.

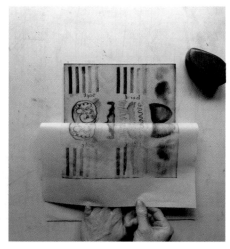

Pulling back the hand-printed impression reveals the result.

Results from Hand Printing and by Press

The results clearly show the difference in quality and expression of marks produced from the press and by hand. It is easy to say that the one printed under the press is stronger, but that is not always true. Hand printing allows the artist to apply pressure at different levels across the matrix, giving more control in the resultant impression. It can create a very atmospheric print and means that you are not dictated in scale by the size of your press bed. Choose when to use each method and why.

A FEW MARKS OUTSIDE THE BOX

The traditional lithographic tools used in a standard manner will produce quite predictable results. This is not a negative thing, just a predictable one. A crayon mark will probably, if etched and printed well, look like a crayon mark. There are a few ways to approach the grease-based mark-making that can be slightly more experimental. I have printed a tester piece demonstrating a few such examples. It has been created on a birch ply matrix and printed under an etching press on smooth Zerkall paper.

Ink Transfer

The ink transfer techniques played with in earlier chapters can be used in reverse to apply ink to the Mokulito plate as

Apply a thin layer of oil-based ink to medium-weight paper.

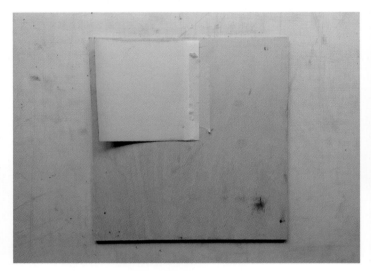

Tape one side of the paper gently in position, ink side down.

Use various tools as described in Chapter 3 to create marks.

An impression created using a few alternative techniques.

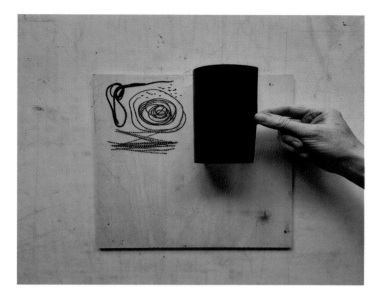

Carefully peel back the inked paper; it can be reused again.

Tape the image down, toner facing down, and brush on acetone.

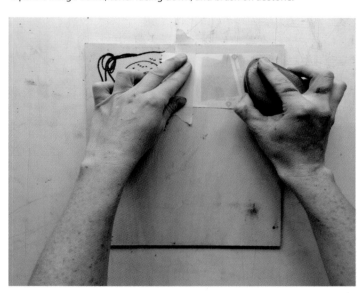

Rub pressure all over, working quickly before the acetone dries.

You can gently check and apply more acetone again if needed.

opposed to the paper. The results are very beautiful and open up a wealth of spontaneous autographic mark-making, which sits in beautiful dialogue with the more graphic wood grain of the Mokulito plate.

Acetone Transfer

The toner from laser jet printers or some old photocopiers is a grease-based toner. This can be utilized in lithography. If you have a printout from a laser jet that you wish to transfer onto a Mokulito plate, you can coat the back with acetone and hand burnish the toner onto the matrix, effectively transferring the grease-based toner onto your matrix. This allows you to transfer text, photographic imagery or any other digital imagery onto the wood, which can be an interesting contrast with the more autographic litho marks. The image choice tends to work best if it is graphic, as you can lose the mid tones in the transfer. You also need to be aware of your wood grain, which can interfere with some of the very fine images. It can be a bit hit and miss and is well worth practising.

Acetone has pretty poor environmental credentials, so use sparingly and in a well-ventilated space. This technique in principle is brilliant and worth exploring, until a more environmentally sound alternative is found.

Stamping

We return again to introducing a relief element to the mark-making. If you use an oil-based printmaking ink, you may apply stamp effects to the surface of the ply. This can involve anything from a home-made stamp, items from around the home with textural surfaces or even a piece of previously carved lino. All these items will need to be inked up following the relief method and stamped onto the ply. Make good use of masks to build up

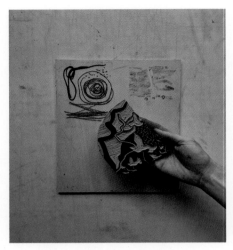

Ink up some lino with standard oil-based ink.

Stamp the lino directly using hand pressure.

Carefully peel back to reveal a clean print.

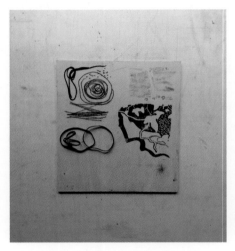

Use unusual materials with oil-based ink to create texture.

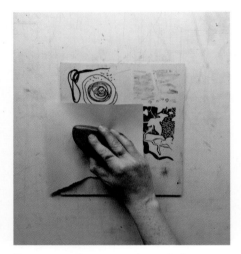

Place a piece of paper over the top before applying pressure.

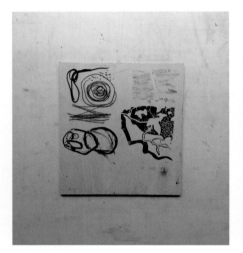

Carefully remove the inky material to reveal the texture.

strong shapes. When etching the ply, make sure the oil-based ink has a good dusting of talc to stop it from smearing when applying the etch.

Using Varnish to Create Textures

Hard wax oils or other similar wood treatments can fill in the wood grain surface of your plate, thus creating a completely different texture to work with when rolling up. By using a water-resistant varnish or paint, you are building up a smooth layer that prevents the usual background plate tone of wood grain from printing. The printed results of the application of such varnishes vary according to which varnishes you use and how you apply them. Here, in the example, I am using a water-resistant hard wax oil applied with a paintbrush. I have applied two coats. The impression has an effect of watercolour, with the slight visual appearance of brush marks. It adds interest and a varying texture to the Mokulito print. Have a play with different

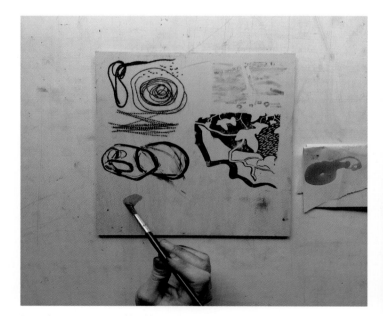

Paint the varnish on and build up to two or three layers.

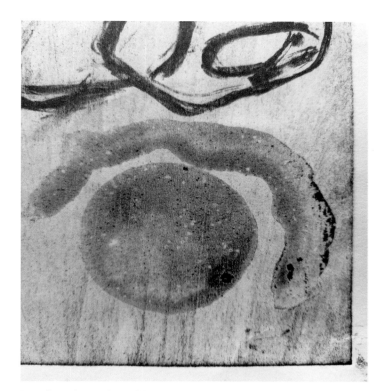
Varnish produces a beautiful ephemeral result when printed.

A stove-top coffee maker is a good way to make distilled water at home.

varnishes and paints to see what effect they have. Always make sure they are bone dry before running under an etching press otherwise the pressure will 'pop' any areas of damp varnish and your paper will stick.

Reticulation

If you have ever read about or done any lithography, you will have probably heard this term mentioned. It describes an effect created through the drying of a grease wash on the surface of your matrix. As the wash dries, the grease will create tide marks, similar to the tide marks up the side of a bath after slowly draining dirty water. Depending on what media you use to generate your wash, the tide marks will appear in different formations. This effect is known as reticulation and is specific to lithography. You are advised to work with distilled water to create the washes and reticulated effects. Tap water may have impurities that will affect the way the grease settles upon the surface of the wood. You can use a clean stove-top coffee maker to make a small batch of distilled water by setting it up as you would to make coffee, but without the coffee added.

It is a beautiful effect and one that you can spend hours on to try to perfect. Mokulito has a wood grain to work with, so you have to be aware of this and understand the finest of reticulated marks may not be possible. However, textures

The basic materials needed to work with reticulated washes.

Rub the stick tusche in a plate to transfer a grease layer.

Add some distilled water and mix until the tusche dissolves.

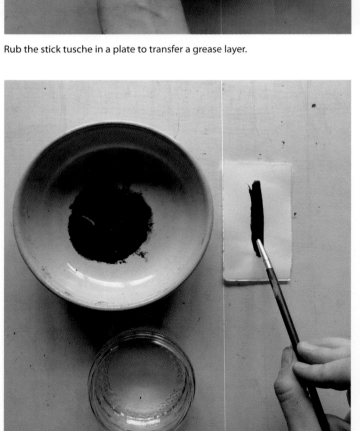

Test the solution on paper to make sure it is a dark grey.

Add drops of liquid tusche in water puddles and leave to spread and dry.

An inked-up section of Tetra Pak with some monoprint marks.

The Tetra Pak was printed ink side down onto the surface of the wood.

and tonal washes are possible and certainly something to play with. I work with a stick tusche to create tonal washes and reticulation. If you use a maple veneer ply or a solid maple, then this will give you a good chance of picking up finer detail, whereas a birch ply would mean that more plate grain is incorporated. It is all about having a play with the washes and surface.

Monoprint Transfer

Transferring a monoprint onto the surface of the Mokulito plate works very successfully. Using the techniques previously discussed, it works best using a piece of Tetra Pak or a sheet of True Grain/drafting film. The monoprint marks will be competing with the wood grain, but the general impression is successful.

Materia Prima, Danielle Creenaune.

Editioning

Mokulito can produce a small edition, depending on the wood chosen for the matrix and the marks added, alongside a bit of luck from the litho gods. Every time you wish to print a fresh impression, the matrix needs to be re-inked following the standard procedure. As this occurs, the wood grain fills in more and the lithographic marks lose their clarity. Thus, as the edition progresses, the balance between wood grain and lithographic marks shifts to favour the wood grain. It is down to artistic preference at which point in the edition process is the preferred balance, and in some cases it may be stronger to have more wood grain showing. Woods such as maple fill in less quickly than birch ply.

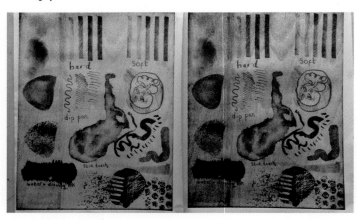

The first pull on the left and the sixth pull on the right, with more in-fill.

A birch ply Mokulito plate after the sixth edition showing signs of grain in-fill.

PROJECT

INTEGRATING WOODCUT

Mokulito has that wonderful benefit of being able to turn into a woodcut as well as a lithograph. The woodcut can be worked at any stage after the gum has been added, or before the drawing is applied. It is difficult to work the woodcut marks during the drawing process since it risks smudging the greasy lithographic marks. You can even print your matrix as a Mokulito with no woodcut, then carve back into the matrix once you have completed your impressions and over print the woodcut back onto the lithographic impression. It opens up some wonderfully expressive potential.

This fun project is designed to guide you through creating a basic Mokulito and woodcut piece, so that you can begin to get to grips with the process and potentials. We are using a still life of fruit as our inspiration. I have chosen one whole (windfall) apple, one fig cut in half and two fig leaves. It is created using solid side-grain cherry as the Mokulito base.

Foraging Dance, Mary Dalton. This Mokulito was printed upon birch ply with woodcut added. It was printed under an etching press on damp paper. The boldness of the image shows that Mokulito can be both tonal and full of washes as well as more graphic.

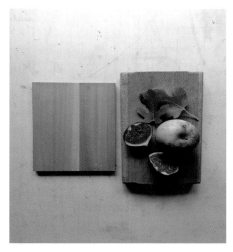

The chosen still life and solid cherry wood for the Mokulito.

Starting out with washes to give a loose drawing impression.

Using traditional litho materials to add texture and tone.

Using the ink transfer technique adds some spontaneous marks.

Use of a mask allows you to create cut forms to work within.

Try hand stamping inked up surfaces for a change of dynamics.

Build up the image slowly using varying tools and techniques.

Areas of varnish should be the last layer, to allow it to dry.

Integrating woodcut into a Mokulito is very rewarding. It can add some graphic areas of clean white, with no possibility of plate grain showing. You can also play with the cut marks to add emboss and texture in the print. Check your tools are sharp and suitable for wood. Note also that each timber will cut differently. Some, such as basic birch ply, provide more resistance against the grain and can risk splintering; others with a tighter grain such as the cherry I am using here, cut more smoothly against the grain.

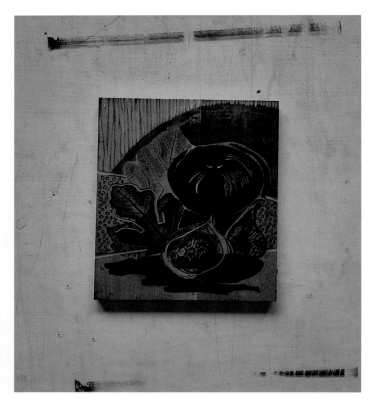
The matrix ready to print using damp paper under the press.

After etching with gum as normal, woodcut marks can be added.

Rolling up the cleaned and dampened Mokulito with black ink.

The completed impression combining Mokulito with woodcut.

UNUSUAL APPROACHES

We have established the basic Mokulito and woodcut process and it is pretty special. There are a few ways in which we can, let's say, spice things up a little. Here are a few suggestions.

Use a Fretsaw

A fretsaw is a wonderful tool that allows you to cut intricate details and tight curves into the wooden matrix. As soon as you are able to cut up your timber so readily, you no longer need to have it as a square-edged impression. The saw allows you to change the edge of the matrix or make many jigsaw pieces that you ink up and reconfigure together on the press bed. This means that each little piece can be treated differently in the inking process, perhaps inked with different colours. It can have a range of different drawing marks applied or different woodcut marks, all without affecting its neighbour. You can cut before or after the drawing stage, depending on how you wish to work, either responding to marks already drawn or cutting pre-designed elements. If cutting after the drawing stage, it is advisable to gum up first to protect your marks from sawdust and smudging. Edges can then be sanded smooth prior to printing. The fretsaw method also allows you to integrate a Mokulito shape into another printing method as a free-form element. It allows for much hybridization.

A fretsaw is used to cut curves and shapes in the timber.

Clamp down your matrix using scrap card to protect the wood.

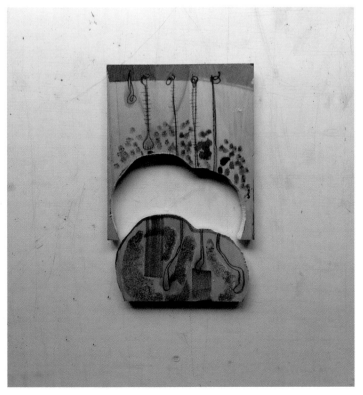

An example of cutting the matrix producing independent parts.

Different Wood

We have been working on standard birch ply up to this point, because it is the most readily available and cost effective. I have done some tests on alternative woods, which are highlighted below. All of these are still side-grain timber – that is, they are taken from a plank running down the length of the tree, not across the tree. They are also all solid timber, which if sourced from correctly managed forests, is a more sustainable environmental approach then the production of ply.

A solid plank of timber that is less than 10mm in depth will be prone to warping when the wet gum is applied. This will usually flatten out under a press so is not too much of a problem.

Some of the timbers that are referred to as solid are actually slim planks of solid timber glued together with the grain going in opposing directions. This helps negate the warping.

As far as these different timbers go, maple works stunningly well with Mokulito. It has little background grain and produces great washes. It struggles, as some other timbers do, to etch litho crayon or tablet, but the other marks print beautifully. You can buy solid maple as I am using here, or you can buy maple-veneered ply. Both are a more costly investment than birch ply, but the results are significantly more stable. Other timbers will scum up very quickly, such as the elm tested here, and some will have a distinctive grain, such as ash. The latter

A selection of solid timber planks. From left to right: elm, maple, ash.

The three solid planks with tester marks drawn on. From left to right: elm, maple, ash.

After the gum etch is applied, the planks less than 10 mm have some warping. It flattens under a press.

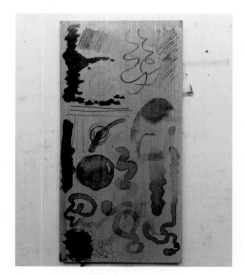

Solid maple inked up and ready to print. It is very clear to see the beautiful subtleties of the washes the timber can produce, with very little background grain. Note that the litho crayon and pencil marks at the top have not etched as clearly. This is common.

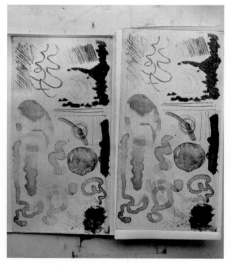

Two impressions pulled from the maple tester matrix. The washes have gained in strength on the second impression, right.

A detail showing the delicate wash marks that maple is capable of picking up.

Ash timber produces a strong grain, which affects the marks drawn on. It can be quite beautiful if worked with rather than against.

The ash impression pulled from the tester plate shows a strong grain.

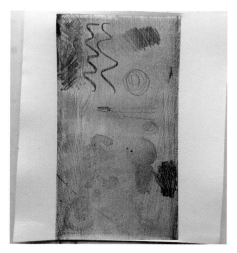

The impression from the elm timber shows the full in-fill of the background. Some timbers are just not suited for Mokulito; it is worth trying and experimenting.

can be very interesting if worked with knowing it will print a strong grain.

Colour

Mokulito can be inked up in colour. It is as simple as that. There are no changes to the process, just roll up in colour straight over your drawn marks and away you print. You can also apply roll-overs, as we looked at in Chapter 4. The only issue with applying a roll-over is that it stops the Mokulito from being editioned. As soon as you add a background of oil-based ink over the inked up Mokulito, you are unable to clean that roll-over ink off for subsequent editions. It prints beautifully, so perhaps it is worth trying at the end of an edition run? Or just taking that bold leap into producing a unique print, the approach I tend to roll with. It's far more fun!

Colour Added by Watercolour

Mokulito is very good at receiving hand-painted watercolour onto the surface of the wood. It has to be added after inking with your oil-based ink and whilst the ply is still ever so slightly damp. Try not to pool watercolour onto the surface of the plate, particularly near any wood cut marks. What can happen is that the watercolour will seep into the woodcut marks, and they will not print cleanly white if printed under a press. Work reasonably dry with the watercolour and you will get some wonderful results. It is crucial that you print onto damp paper, and although the technique will work by hand, it works with greater strength of colour under a press. The results are satisfying and direct.

Blue Falls, Danielle Creenaune. A beautiful example of a Mokulito being inked up and printed in blue. As we looked at earlier in the book, blue is very good at translating fine details and softer layers.

Use a soft brush to apply areas of watercolour onto the wood.

After you have made your woodcut marks and your matrix is inked and ready to print, add a piece of clean tissue paper cut to the shape and size you wish for the blind emboss area. Place this over the top of the blind emboss section of the Mokulito matrix and print as standard.

Re-Sanding Matrices

Like all lithography methods, you are able to re-use your wooden matrix, to an extent. Once the inky marks are completely dry, you can re-sand the surface to remove all the greasy marks and start over. This process works better on solid timber rather than ply, since the ply top layer is so thin, it does not take much to sand through to the next layer. You do not need to use white spirit or turpentine to remove any previously drawn imagery. Just let the whole lot dry completely and sand away, starting with a medium grade and heading down to a very fine grade and finally finish with a fine wire wool.

The print with watercolour areas being pulled from the press.

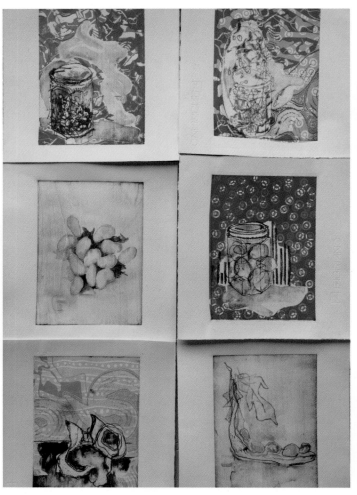
Preparing for Winter (series), Mary Dalton. A series of Mokulito prints all created from re-sanded solid wood matrices. The Mokulito is the monochrome drawing and linocut was added for the colour.

Blind Emboss

We have looked at the blind emboss previously, and it makes a return in Mokulito. If you choose to integrate woodcut marks to your plate, you have the option of creating a blind emboss with them which offers a wonderful contrast to the rest of the print. It works best under a press with high pressure.

MOKULITO IN ITS FULL GLORY

The following project is aimed at encompassing a bit of everything we can in terms of Mokulito, but applying these elements with thought and consideration. In the demonstration, the print is a unique print since there will be a roll-over involved. If you wish to play further with the plates you create, then I suggest you do not use a roll-over. The subject matter is free. I will be working on birch ply and printing under a press for the Mokulito, but printing by hand for the woodcut addition. The starting size of my ply is 20 × 30cm.

The print and the plate will be having time to dry between impressions. You will see this mentioned in the process. This is quite important if you wish for clear imagery and clarity of colour. Be patient: it should not take too long since the lithography layer is such a thin film of ink, and it can sometimes dry in a few hours. If you are limited with time, then go ahead and print without drying, but just note the difference.

NAGGING PROBLEMS

Mokulito can be sensitive, and it takes a bit of practice to work out why some things may not be working as you expect. To help, we shall go over a few of the most common issues and their potential solutions. The key is to remember that if you give

The ink transfer method is a great way to start the drawing.

Using paper masks allows for controlled forms when required.

Utilize the paper dry-point card to transfer textured forms.

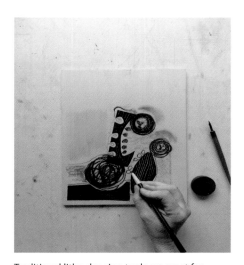

Traditional litho drawing tools are great for detailed areas.

Use masks to create expressive texture within defined forms.

Hand-stamping inked lino can add bold contrast in the work.

Think where to add gentle washes for contrast and subtlety.

Dust gently with talc and etch the matrix using gum Arabic.

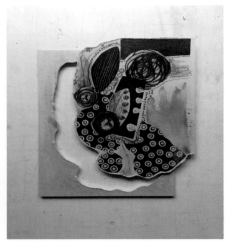

Make any coping saw interventions after the gum is bone dry.

Using carving tools, woodcut marks are added prior to inking.

After washing, roll up the damp matrix using oil-based ink.

Apply any coloured roll-overs to elements prior to printing.

Place masks on the matrix for areas of white or blind emboss.

The last layer before printing is any watercolour additions.

The completed Mokulito done in a single pull under a press.

time to lithography, it will return the patience and love tenfold. Never give up.

Scumming Up

Scumming up describes when you roll up a prepared matrix and instead of the non-image areas remaining clean, they in-fill with ink and 'scum up'. This could happen for a number of reasons, but there are a few to eliminate before you put it down to a dodgy piece of timber, which can happen.

Firstly, too much ink. Mokulito needs a thin layer of ink when used in conjunction with a rubber roller. It is thicker than a roll-over layer and you need to hear a light hiss.

Secondly, the ink is too oily. The ink needs to be marginally looser than straight out of the tube, but you also want to make sure it is not too loose. If you feel this may be the problem, scrape up your ink and start the viscosity mixing again. You can also add a touch of French chalk to ink to stiffen it.

Thirdly, the matrix is too dry. This will inevitably mean the non-image areas ink up. Squeeze water all over the matrix, wipe evenly and roll-over in quick light actions to snap off any background ink.

Washes Filling In

Lithography is very sensitive to grease. If you have created a beautiful tonal work on the matrix, sometimes when it comes to inking, it will just fill in with black ink. When layering all the washes, although separated and tonal on the matrix, the wood will just understand these washes as layers of grease upon grease, which will therefore just print black. They key is to keep washes high in contrasting tonal value, and to not layer up too much. This should allow you to generate a nice layering effect when inking.

Tramlines

Tramlines can be a nuisance when inking Mokulito. These are negated through good rolling technique with the rubber roller or using a roller wider than one side of your matrix. The latter is a simple solution, but not always practical considering tools available. Good rolling technique can negate tram lines completely. The key is to use a firm and quick pressure with your roller to start with, and then snap off any tramlines with quick light pressure across the plate. You can also squeeze water directly onto the tramlines before you snap them off with the roller. Tramlines can be removed without having to resort to a sponge roller and it is always prudent to practise good rolling actions.

Paper Sticking

Paper can sometimes stick to the Mokulito matrix after printing under a press, which can cause peeling and damage to the impression. This may be due to some heavily inked areas, some litho crayon still on the plate, or even some gum not washed off fully. The best way to eradicate this is to print onto dry paper rather than damp. If you are printing under a high-pressured press then you will still get a very strong impression.

A plate that was too dry before rolling – the ink has scummed up the background.

A delicate hand and an awareness of wash strengths will serve you well.

CHAPTER 6

LITHINO

Lithino is a technique of printmaking that has developed alongside knowledge of Mokulito and traditional stone lithography. It allows the artist to turn a lino matrix into a lithographic one, at any stage of a linocut. The lino picks up lithographic details incredibly well and allows the artist to work on scales that traditional stone lithography might restrict, due to the materials or the technical press requirements. It can be hand printed or printed under a press. Unlike Mokulito on ply, where the artist may make only one image before the matrix is spent, the lino plate can be prepared at any point during its printed life to receive lithographic marks. The bold autographic marks of lithography combine beautifully with the crisp graphic marks of a linocut and the results are quite astounding. It suits itself to combining with other print-making methods already discussed in this book, and offers huge expressive potential for unique printmaking. This chapter will introduce you to the basic process of Lithino.

WHY DEVELOP LITHINO?

Lithino was first developed as a way of breaking from the graphic constraints of a classic linocut. There are many ways in which artists are able to introduce more expressive, autographic marks into a linocut, but none really meet the criteria of direct mark-making. A caustic soda etch upon the lino surface creates textural effects, but it is still quite indirect and based upon a carved and non-carved relationship. Furthermore, the caustic soda is hugely damaging for the environment. Dremels, graters, sandpaper and many alternative tools can also create energetic marks, but again, they are restricted by the resistance of the lino surface itself. The idea of introducing a lithographic mark onto the lino enables a direct drawn mark to be made unhindered.

The lino surface is processed so it becomes silky smooth to draw on, unlike Mokulito, where the wood grain offers an input in any mark made. The lino surface is more akin to drawing on a lithographic stone surface, which offers a wonderful autographic experience for the artist.

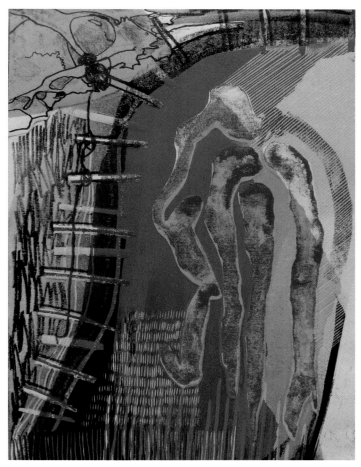

A detail from a complex lithino print.

Lithino can be printed by hand or under any etching press, direct drive or geared. It can be printed with standard hard rubber printmaking rollers, in monochrome and colour, and picks up beautiful detail true to the original mark.

The principles of applying lithographic techniques to lino stem back to the 1970s. It was initially developed using harsh acids to etch the lino, but with research, new methods have come about. These new, more gentle methods produce incredible results, and what is even more interesting from an artistic perspective is that the artist is able to prepare the lino surface to act lithographically at any stage of a reduction linocut. This means that I could be carving layer number three of a linocut, I can then add lithographic marks on layer number four, and then continue carving on layer five. You may have printed eight layers of a reduction lino, but then wish to add a reticulated wash into the print. This is entirely possible and allows you to slip from lino to litho to lino to litho in any order and any sequence within a print. Naturally, this lends itself to unique and dynamic printmaking, where methods from other chapters in this book can also be integrated, such as collage, stamped lino or monoprint lithographic marks. At any point you can switch back to a traditional lino, perhaps finally dropping in a lithographic crayon layer. The potential for mixed media printing is huge and extremely exciting.

The very first lithino test print.

HOW DOES IT WORK?

As we understood with Mokulito, the principles of any lithographic process rely upon oil and water resisting. Thus, it is imperative that the non-image areas of a lithographic matrix are able to stay damp when sponging, so that the oil-based ink rolled over is repelled from this surface and only attracted to the greasy drawn marks. The surface of traditional lino is actually marginally water repellent. It is a great flooring surface for kitchens and bathrooms, where water spillages occur frequently and the lino happily resists them. You can test for yourself by brushing clean water over the surface with a wide bristle brush. The water does not stay true to the brush mark, but gathers into water droplets and pools. Great for flooring, but in lithographic terms, this causes problems because the artist would be unable to create an even damp film across the lino surface when sponging down – which, as we know, is essential to good lithographic printing.

To prevent the pooling effect, a plate grain needs to be added to the print matrix to allow micro-droplets of water to be held evenly across the surface. To create the plate grain on lino the solution is so simple: it needs sanding. The process of sanding creates a plate grain on the lino surface that allows it to hold moisture evenly without pooling. The result is clear if, after following the sanding process, you apply a brush mark of clean water. The water no longer pools, but keeps the shape of the brush mark.

Through this simple process, the lino is ready to receive lithographic marks. During the research process, after a drawing

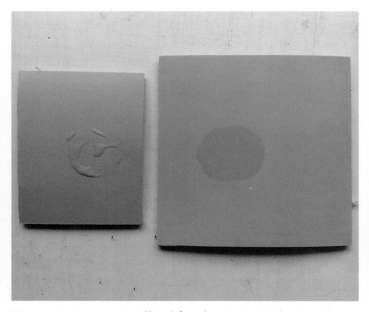

Water separating on untreated lino, left, and staying in a pool on treated lino, right.

had been created with a range of lithographic tools, it was vital to test if the lino would react to a gum Arabic etch. It did and it worked beautifully. The following project will introduce you to the basic process of lino preparation and printing. From there, we will explore how it can be integrated into a reduction linocut, how we can work with colour and how it can be worked with the other techniques we have discussed in the book thus far.

Materials

The lithographic set up with regards to drawing tools and workshop is the same as in Chapter 5: Mokulito. Additional tools are listed below. Again, as discussed in Mokulito, some household grease-based drawing tools may be used, and these will need to be experimented with by the artist. The lithino can be printed by hand or by etching press; we will look at both in this chapter.

- Lino
  This needs to be the traditional jute-backed artist's lino. The grey variety is the most stable and easiest to work with this technique. Two A4 sheets should suffice for the projects here.
- Lino cutting tools
  A basic set will cover your needs in this chapter.
- Sandpaper and wire wool

Traditional lithography materials and grey lino work well in combination.

Sandpaper of very fine grade, which is usually 240 grit, and some wire wool of fine grade will cover your needs.
- Printing barren
  A wooden spoon or Japanese printing barren will do a great job.
- Paper
  A selection of printmaking papers of different weights is useful. If printing under a press, you can go as high as 220 gms printing paper. If printing by hand, I would advise a Japanese paper no heavier than 120 gms. As always, A4 print out paper or basic cartridge is a great means to test. You need to use paper with as smooth a surface as possible to help pick up the details.
- Wide, soft bristled brush
- Scalpel/Stanley knife and cutting mat
- Double-sided tape
- Face covering/mask
  You will be sanding lino, so it is best to wear a mask.

PROJECT

PREPARING AND PROCESSING THE LINO LITHOGRAPHICALLY

This introductory project will cover how we turn the lino matrix into a lithographic one. This print will purely be a tester print so that you may understand how certain marks print and react to the lino surface. Sanding is the crucial element in this process, and it can take a bit of time, but it is essential, so be patient with it. Even if lino is inert to humans, please do wear a face mask/covering to avoid breathing in any lino dust. If you can, work in a ventilated area or even outside.

This project piece is a sampler, so make sure that you note down any marks you like so that you do not forget how they were made. Try to test out a full range of marks and lithographic processes, including washes. You will notice that the lino surface is completely different to draw on in comparison to a wooden Mokulito surface. There is very little resistance to drawn marks, thus enabling a more fluid drawing. There will be a marginal plate tone when printing the lino, particularly at the edges so remember this when laying down marks near the edge. Gentle washes and fine details have a greater chance of printing clearly than the same marks produced upon a Mokulito matrix.

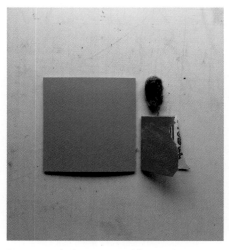

To prepare the lino you need fine sandpaper and wire wool.

Rub the sandpaper in even strokes across the lino surface.

Sand the lino from different directions to ensure an even grain.

Carefully sand the edges to create a smooth, curved edge.

Finish with the wire wool to produce a silky, even surface.

Brush off loose lino dust using a clean, soft-bristled brush.

Fully test the lithographic materials on the lino surface.

Feel how drawing with litho ink works on the smooth surface.

Test out all grades of tonal washes, from faint to strong.

Play with how tusche washes and reticulation respond to lino.

The completed test sheet has a full range of marks to print.

Drawing onto the Surface

The lino should feel like silk to the touch, very appealing and wondrous. Try to avoid touching the surface too much because this could lay grease down on the surface and etch as a positive mark. When drawing on the surface of the lino, make sure the lino is as flat as possible. You can slightly bend the lino so that it does lay flat or warm it over a radiator to relax the oils so that it levels off. If the lino is not level when creating wash work, your water will puddle and gather in one spot, affecting the reticulation and grease content.

Etching

Etching the lino surface is slightly different from traditional lithography. It is an important stage, so take your time and have all the relevant materials ready to go – talc, cloth for talc distribution, gum Arabic and the wide bristle brush. Make sure that all water-based washes and inks are completely dry on the surface of the lino. Once the gum is on, you will need to leave the lino undisturbed for at least two days. Exposure to natural sunlight and warmth can help, but time is the crucial element. After the first application of gum, you may need to return to the lino half an hour or so later, to gently brush over the surface to even out any pooling of gum.

Printing

Printing lithino is so incredibly satisfying. It holds detail very well, and if the etch was successful, then it also prints and rolls up with a fair amount of stability allowing you to, if you wish, create a small edition. At the printing stage, I am going to demonstrate using both a spring-top etching press and printing by hand. If you are able, I would advise the same, as the results are quite different and offer the artist options within

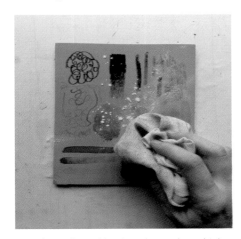
Dust the surface with talc and spread out thinly and evenly.

Apply a thick, but even layer, of gum Arabic across the lino.

Check you have not missed areas and leave to etch in daylight.

expressive potentials. Make sure you select the right paper for the correct process. If using a printing press, I would suggest a heavy printmaking paper, such as Fabriano Rosaspina 220 gms. This will enable you to see the quality of the mark on a professional standard printmaking paper. Although lithino does print very well on dry paper, you can also surface dampen the paper to pick up further mid tones. You will need to be aware, as with Mokulito, if you dampen the paper, it can marginally stretch and shrink, which may affect any subsequent layers. You do not want to set the press pressure too high, as this could potentially stretch the lino out of shape. Please do use lino runnes to help raise up your rollers. If you are printing on heavier weight papers, note that you may need to print the subsequent lino layers also under a press because the hand printing of lino through thick paper can be tough. If you wish

to try to print more than one, the lino will need re-dampening and rolling up again before the next print. If remaining stable, lithino can print over ten prints.

If printing by hand, then you need to work with a lightweight paper, anywhere from 30 gms to 120 gms. This enables you to print the litho layer and the lino layer by hand with ease. You will be working with dry paper for this process.

Results and Development

The sampler of the lithographic layer on the lino is quite beautiful and very different from a Mokulito sampler. The first thing to note is that there is little plate tone from the lino surface. The edges may have a little ink gather – this is not uncommon in lithography – but the background tone is relatively clean. If printing a Mokulito, you are working with the grain of the

Remove the gum from the lino under a tap and with a sponge.

Evenly dampen the lino surface in preparation for rolling up.

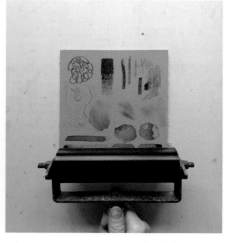
Roll up with a thin layer of black ink, firmly and quickly.

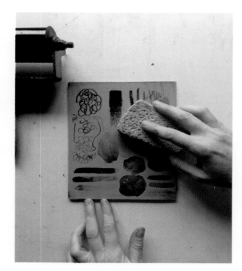
Keep the lino damp at all times by sponging over the surface.

The lithino is ready to print under an etching press.

The lithino print shows the fine details you can pick up.

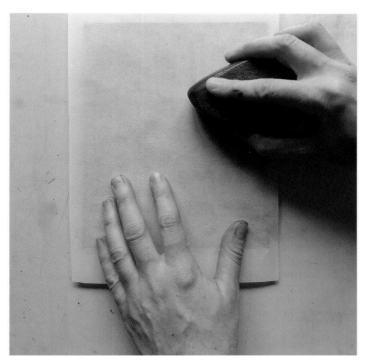

Placing 39 gms dry Japanese paper down on the inked lithino.

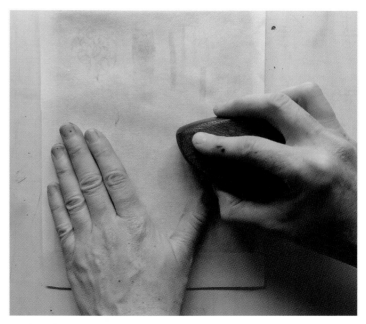

Applying firm pressure all over with the wooden hand barren.

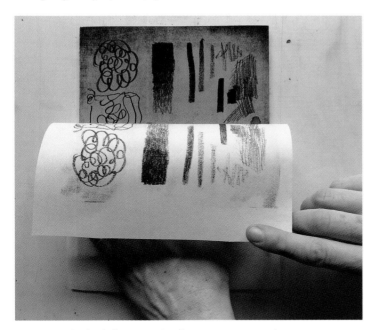

You can gently check the impression for pressure as you print.

The hand printed impression is fainter but still very strong.

timber integrated both in your marks and potentially in the background (depending on the timber you choose). This is what makes Mokulito so appealing and unique. With a lithino mark, the smooth lino surface allows for no interruption to the more gentle washes, reticulated marks, smudges and pen work. Thus they print very true and clean. The crayon and drawing ink marks roll up well, which sometimes struggle to pick up on a Mokulito. Everything is printed very true to what was drawn, which is exciting.

The print created on the press holds a lot more detail, particularly the damp paper version, which lends itself to picking up very fine washes. The hand-printed version on Japanese 39 gms paper has a very ephemeral quality. The rich blacks may be lost, but another distinct dream-like quality is apparent, which is rather unique.

Sanding Grain

In traditional stone lithography, the artist has a choice of adding a textured grain to the surface of the stone before they commence drawing. This grain will change the quality of the overall drawing, from, for instance, a smooth, even tone to a speckled tone. The intensity of the speckle depends on the grain that has been added. In lithino, we can do the same. Once the lino has an overall even sand, you can re-sand the lino with a rough sandpaper to add a scratchy or speckled effect to any subsequent lithographic marks. The sanding should remain very shallow and should not affect any subsequent lino layers. The thicker layer of ink laid down for the relief work should in-fill the scratches. If not, you can always re-sand the lino with a fine grade sandpaper and wire wool to help remove, or at least lessen, the previous plate grain added.

Drawing onto the surface of the lino with lithographic tools.

Applying a textured grain to the lino with coarse sandpaper.

Checking the strength, direction and evenness of the grain.

The printed impression showcases a wonderful grainy texture.

OUTSIDE DRAWING

Having established how we draw lithographically onto the lino, we are now going to look at the potentials of this technique in the wider view of printmaking. In this project we will be working outside, drawing our lithographic marks directly and intuitively in response to the environment around us. We will then be introducing a linocut layer that is worked in response to the lithographic marks. The combination of all of this will highlight the huge potential of this technique.

Working outside is very easy with this lithographic technique: all you need is the lino and your lithographic drawing tools. The setting is your choice – it can be anywhere from a local woodland to a back garden. We will be working in a free manner, using the autographic potential of the lithographic tools to gesturally represent the environment rather than replicate it. To showcase the contrast between the gestural lithographic marks and the graphic lino carving, I would advise you to cover most of your matrix with lithographic texture, even if we end up covering it with solid black later down the line. At this stage of learning about the process, it is better to have more options of textures to work with than too few.

The lithographic stage will require a few days under etch before we return to print it and add lino carving. Both hand

A simple outside garden in early winter offers much interest.

Make sure you have your materials to hand before you start.

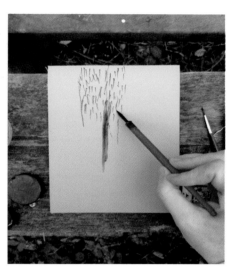

Draw freely with movement without representing exact imagery.

Gestural and bold washes add huge energy and life to works.

Think about what varying textures you wish to add and where.

The completed lithino drawing will need to dry undisturbed.

printing and press printing work well for this project, or a combination of the two, as I will be demonstrating.

Lino Cutting and Printing

After the etch has sat for a few days, you are ready to print following the process explained earlier. I am printing mine onto surface dampened Fabriano Rosaspina 220 gms underneath a direct drive etching press. The lino layer is going to be hand printed as I wish to integrate some hand printing effects.

After the lithographic layer is printed and you have enough copies to play with, you will need to remove the ink from

The drawing is rolled up as previously, with black ink.

The lithographic print is printed under an etching press.

Carving into the lino using the lithographic marks to guide.

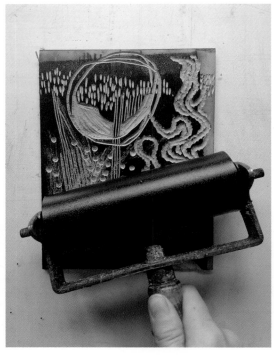

Rolling up the carved linocut with oil-based black ink.

The impression showing the bold combination of litho and lino.

Tusche Effects

The basic water tusche reticulated wash can already print interesting marks and contours. But if you are to add some other materials to the washes as they dry, you can create some other textural results. Salt and baking powder are two great examples, and they are well worth trying. Lithino has no plate grain to interfere with these more delicate marks, so they stand a greater chance of producing a clean impression then if they were created on a Mokulito surface. The details of these washes are best picked up on damp paper under a press, but you can pick up the general atmosphere through hand printing.

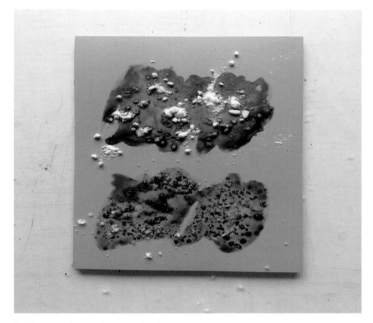

Baking powder (top) and rock salt sprinkled on tusche washes.

the surface of the lino with a clean rag and a tiny amount of vegetable oil alongside a fair amount of rubbing. You want to avoid getting a lot of oil on the surface of the lino as it can affect the inking up of the lino layer and also any subsequent lithographic layers. You will not be able to remove all the lithographic drawing marks, and this is actually very useful as they offer you a guide as to where you wish to carve. They will not print. You may then proceed with the lino carving.

MORE COMPLEX EFFECTS

The previous project highlights that there are some stunning combinations of marks when lithography is combined with lino. Many of the strongest marks come from not even trying, the ones that occur without planning and that may well be labelled as mistakes. These are the ones that often sing.

Reticulation, the wonderful effect we talked briefly about in Mokulito, is more stable when printing on lino. Unlike in Mokulito where a wood grain can interrupt reticulation, lino has a smooth surface, so the beautiful tide marks of grease left behind as the water evaporates are very clear. There are some fun effects to be had in a reticulated water wash, which print beautifully under a press.

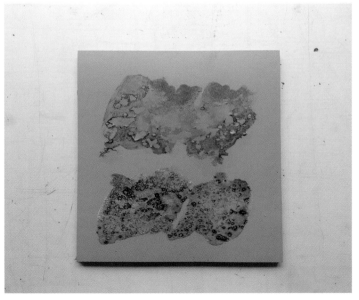

After the tusche is dry, loose powder is gently brushed off.

Gum is applied carefully to avoid dislodging stuck-on particles.

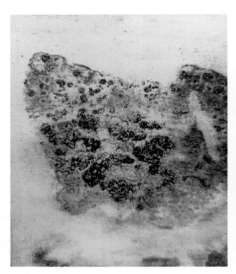

The impression taken from the rock salt wash is very textural.

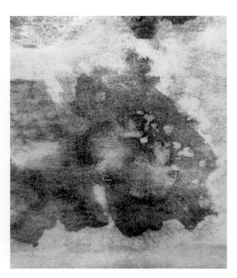

The impression taken from the baking powder wash is very soft.

Gum Arabic Resists

This is a brilliant technique that is specific to lithography. We have learnt that the gum Arabic reacts with the non-image areas of the lino and creates a surface that can remain damp upon roll-up. This can be utilized across the lino surface to part-etch areas, and allow other areas to in-fill with the black ink upon rolling. It makes more sense when demonstrated, and holds many possibilities for expression.

You can also use gum Arabic to create masks. The gum can be painted directly onto prepared lino to block out areas as you work around other areas. The gum protects whatever is underneath it from the greasy tool, in essence, acting like a mask. You can freely draw over the gum to allow continuity of marks across the lino, but you cannot use water-based washes near it, since the water dissolves the gum mask.

Monochrome Greys

A lithographic impression contains a much finer layer of printing ink than a linocut relief impression. You will have seen the difference in this when inking up the lithographic layer and the lino layer. It is worth accentuating this to an extent if printing a two-tone monochrome print, as in our first project. If you mix a lovely charcoal grey and use this to print the first litho layer and then print the lino layer in a solid black, your print will leap

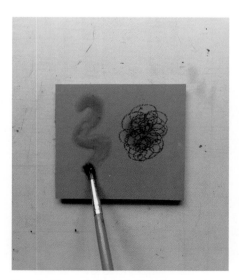

Gum Arabic applied neat (left) and as a mask over drawing (right).

Once dry, further drawn marks are applied over the masked section.

After etching, washing and rolling up, the results are clear.

Cutting the Ivy, Mary Dalton. A large scale (100 × 100cm) lithino with charcoal grey litho layer and black lino layer. The grey litho layer adds energy and autographic marks to contrast with the bold, black linocut.

A monoprint created on Tetra Pak transferred under a press onto the lino.

off the pages. The layering of the two is quite special and the softer grey of the litho layer really allows the drawn quality of the marks to sing.

Adding a Monoprint

The sensitive surface of the lino responds very well to fine detail and tone. Because the lino can be put under a press, we can use the prepared surface as a recipient for a monoprint, using the technique explored in Chapter 3. Transferring a monoprint onto the surface of the prepared lino is simple, yet hugely effective, and it allows you to integrate the monoprint with the traditional lithographic drawing tools, creating a wonderful visual conversation. You will need to leave a tiny bit more ink upon the monoprint to allow for transfer onto the lino and some of the faintest areas may not fully transfer. Compensate by being bolder with the marks you create.

Colour

Printing a lithino in colour is just as with a Mokulito. When it comes to the inking up stage, the colour required is rolled directly onto the lino surface and then printed. The black of the crayon or washes should not influence the ink being printed.

INTRODUCING LAYERS

Unlike Mokulito, lithino allows you to introduce a lithographic mark at any stage of the linocut. This is quite ground-breaking and extremely exciting with regards to producing dynamic, expressive prints. It primarily works well with a reduction linocut, the lino technique discussed in Chapter 2. Upon any one of these carved layers, you can introduce lithography marks, print, and then return to carving. Suddenly, the lino becomes alive as the autographic lithography marks sing in between the graphic lino marks. It is truly wonderful.

The process is relatively simple, it just requires a little time and attention to the lino surface. When you wish to add some lithographic marks, you will need to remove residual ink with a light oil and rag and then sand the lino surface as before. It is key that the sanded lino surface returns to a uniform colour, with no residual ink staining from previous layers. Any ink from previous printing will etch as a positive mark under the gum Arabic, so it is vital it is gently sanded off. Then the same etching and printing process occurs as before. Once complete, the lino is cleaned and ready to be carved again. If you wish to introduce the lithographic marks to only a small area of the lino, then you need only sand the relevant area. A small demonstration print can showcase how this is achieved, and how complex the end impression can be.

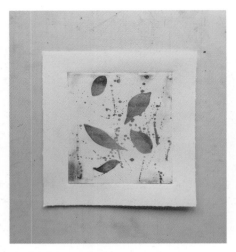

The first lithographic layer printed in crimson under a press.

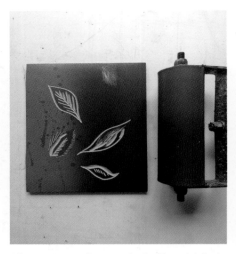

After carving marks away, the lino layer is inked in a blend.

The lino layer is hand printed with a wooden printing barren.

The first stage of the colour lithino printed and left to dry.

Sanding off any residual ink and preparing for the next layer.

Drawing on the next lithography layer onto the prepared lino.

The completed second lithographic layer ready for a gum etch.

Whilst under the dry gum etch, further lino is carved away.

After washing out, the lithino is rolled up in deep orange.

The finished print with two litho layers and two lino layers.

A RETURN TO THE OUTDOOR SCENE, BUT NOT AS YOU SEE IT

This exciting and dynamic project is designed to allow you to understand the gestural and rich marks that lithino can bring to a print. It is designed as a full colour project, working with a single reduction lino matrix. It is suggested to start with a minimum of A4. We will again be working from an outside scene, ideally taking the lino outside, particularly when making the initial lithographic marks, as they can hugely influence the rest of the piece. The colour will be used for both the lithographic areas and lino layers. I am going to be printing under the press for the lithographic layers, to pick up finer detail, and by hand for the lino layers. All will be printed on a smooth Zerkall paper at 145 gms. The project will span several days to allow for litho etching times, so enjoy this and do not rush. It allows for thinking time! It is also crucial to remember to not carve away all the lino at once, since you will need to leave areas to introduce lithographic layers further down the line. Remember, my print is a guide; it is there to help steer, but the interpretation and artistic choices must be yours. That is what makes it unique to you.

The first litho drawing inked up and ready to print.

The first lithographic impression printed under a press.

Carving away into the lino using the litho marks as a guide.

The lino layer printed on top in a transparent orange with a cyan stripe.

The matrix re-sanded and ready for further lithino layers.

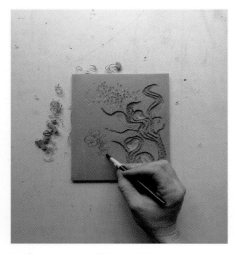

Further carving and lithographic marks are added to the lino.

The lino is part etched with gum Arabic for unique effects.

When fully etched, the lino is washed and rolled up dark green.

The layer is printed and the impression builds in complexity.

After further carving, the lino is rolled up in an opaque white/green mix.

A few tissue paper masks are added to the matrix prior to printing.

The opaque white/green layer blocks out areas of the background.

After further carving additions, the matrix is inked up dark green and more masks placed.

The impression is almost complete.

The matrix is partially sanded, lithographic marks drawn on the specific area, and etched.

Once etched, the lithino is rolled up with a dark blue blend.

The Potential for Cross-Over

Lithino shares many similarities with Mokulito, in as much as it is a lithographic process. However, the ease with which you can re-prepare areas of the plate make it very different in its application. It lends itself to complex layering and colour work, built up in rhythm and harmony with the lino. The lino will respond well to any of the stamping methods used in the first few chapters, as well as some of the monotype transfer methods. This reveals so many beautiful opportunities for complex graphic, yet expressive, prints. It truly is a very exciting medium.

The completed impression is incredibly layered and expressive. The early lithographic marks can be seen through the layers of linocut. The hand printing techniques and masks have added details in between the layers for more depth and interest. When working on a unique print like this, the fun comes through the intuitive building of layers.

CHAPTER 7

COLLAGE IN PRINTMAKING

C ollage has a very important place in printmaking. *Chine-collé* is a term that crops up in many prints, and it is one method of integrating a collaged layer within a printed work. There are other methods, each of which adds its own specific qualities to a print. The principles of layering collage with printed marks is to allow the introduction of a colour, pattern or texture into a work that is not generated through a print matrix. How or when this is introduced is dependent upon the print and technique, but needless to say the possibilities are scrummy. Furthermore, why only rely upon shop-bought collage papers? In this chapter we will look at generating your own patterned and printed papers, which allows you to have a collection of the marks and colours you like. All the processes, from technique through to making will be covered in this chapter.

COLLAGE: CUTTING IT UP AND SHAKING IT UP

Collage can completely change a print. It can add a bold colour, pattern, texture or space that was not conceived in the original matrix. It can allow the artist to freely use a humble pair of scissors as their means to create, not being hindered by print techniques. The boldness of a collaged shape combines beautifully with a printed mark, especially when the collaged paper is integrated seamlessly into the impression. There are a few ways to do this, and we will look at these further into the chapter. You are also able to specify exactly where the collage sits upon the impression, and at which layer. Furthermore, if you print your own collaged papers, it is like slipping in a completely different printed layer into the impression. The freedom this offers is quite immense.

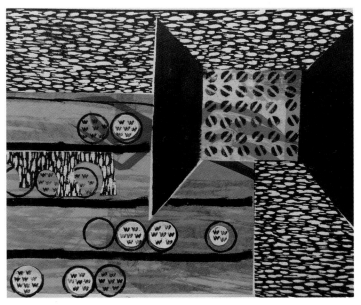

Still Life, Mary Dalton. An example of using collage combined with stamping and linocut. The collage is all the areas of colour, which in themselves are home-made collage papers. They add colour and interest without the need for getting out coloured inks.

Materials

For the projects in this chapter, you will need a selection of papers, as suggested below. You will also need a full set-up of inks and your preferred printing method to generate your own papers. This is entirely up to you – for instance, whether you choose lino, stamping, dry-point – but make sure you have the correct set-up for the methods chosen.

• Japanese paper
  Japanese kozo (or mulberry) papers are extremely strong and make perfect *chine-collé* choices. A Matsuo kozo paper is 16 gms, similar to a standard tissue paper, and comes in many colours. You can also buy other Japanese papers between 9 and 35 gms that would also be suitable. It is worth investing

in a sample pack to appreciate which you prefer before investing in larger quantities.

- Scrap patterned paper
Any type of paper can be used as collage in printmaking, creating a range of different effects. As long as the paper can be glued down, then you can use it as collage. If using a printing press to combine printed impression with collage, try not to use any paper that is heavier than 120 gms. The press will struggle to print an even impression across both the backing paper and the thick collage paper, so a test is advisable. Magazine cuttings, old music scores, patterned bookbinding papers, coloured tissue all work well. It really is just about gathering stock. Avoid newsprint since it is high in acid and yellows very quickly under exposure to sunlight.
- Printmaking paper
You will need this as the backing or impression paper. It needs to be 180 gms or more.
- Nori glue
We will be using traditional rice paste glue for our collage work. It is strong, versatile, archival and cheap. You can buy tubes of it from most paper and print suppliers.
- Tissue paper
- Coloured printing inks and inking set-up
Basic printing set-up and a sheet of clear plastic to fit on your press bed.

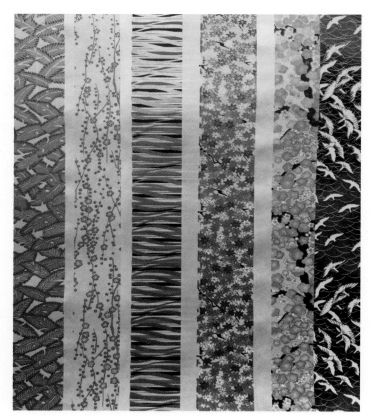

A collection of Chiyogami or patterned Japanese papers.

- Access to an etching press
This is only necessary if you wish to print your own papers; not essential if you are using shop-bought varieties.
- Rice flour
If you wish to make your own rice paste glue, it is simple: you just need rice flour. We will look at how to do this.
- Bone folder
This can be bought very easily in bookbinding stockists and craft suppliers. It allows you to press paper flat, very useful when pasting collage.
- Clean brush and glue container
- Scissors, craft knife and cutting mat
- A selection of print matrices
These are to use as testers to have a play with collage. They could be anything from the previous chapters, for instance, linocut, dry-point or even a set-up for creating a stamped print.

CHINE-COLLÉ

Chine-collé literally translates as China glue. This gives a clue as to the process involved. Thin, traditionally Asian, papers are prepared by the artist with a glue that allows them to bond to the heavier weight backing paper. This bonding process would traditionally occur under the pressure of a press, although it can also be done by hand. The thin fibres of the Asian papers are immensely strong, yet super lightweight. This characteristic allows them to stay coherent with glue, withstand huge pressure and yet bond beautifully with the fibres of the heavier paper. The result is a seamless join between the backing paper and the collage paper, creating a crisp work executed with a high level of craftsmanship.

Chine-collé is not just used for introducing colour or textures. Some Asian papers pick up finer detail then Western paper. A printmaker may actually print their final impression onto a lightweight Japanese paper, then bond this onto a heavier backing paper using the *chine-collé* method. We will be utilizing this principle later in the chapter.

Making *Chine-Collé* Work

Applying *chine-collé* has two main methods. I refer to them as the wet method and the dry method. The wet method involves brushing on fresh glue to the collage paper minutes before bonding it to your paper. The dry method involves preparing your collage papers in advance and re-invigorating the glue prior to printing. Each printmaker is different as to which they prefer and when to use each. We shall look at both, how each is made and when to use each method.

A detail of *chine-collé* in combination with a dry-point.

The materials used for testing the wet method of *chine-collé*.

If you are wishing to overprint the collaged areas, you will need to let the glue dry. Occasionally the wet glue can seep through the thin collage paper and resist the oil-based printing ink, resulting in an uneven impression.

If you are aware that you are wanting to use this method to make a collage base for printing, then it is worth stretching your paper before you start applying glue. This will mean that despite the paper wanting to buckle, it will dry flat.

PROJECT

THE WET METHOD

For this demonstration, a relief print matrix is perfect, for instance some lino. You will also need to select a piece of print-making paper and one piece of thin Japanese collage paper. For this we will be applying one layer of collage and one printed impression, all by hand. We will be using thinned down rice paste glue. It needs to be the consistency of thick gravy. It is a very direct method, and in essence you are literally pasting on the collage before overprinting. This method is not suitable for overprinting with any intaglio method, or a print method that requires printing onto damp paper. The soaking, or direct dampening of the paper, can cause the glue to soften and the collage work to peel away. The dry method is best for intaglio work, and this method is best for relief work or direct stamping.

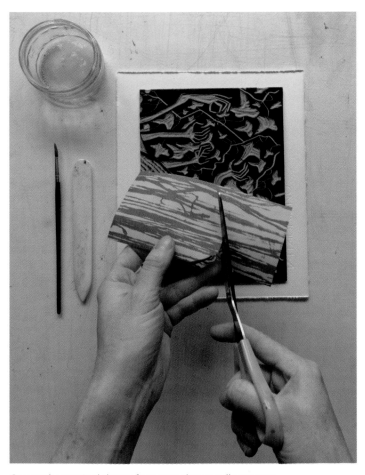

Cut out the required shapes from your chosen collage paper.

Position the collage papers onto your lino.

Gently trace over the collaged shapes and mark the lino edge.

Turn the trace over and rub the marks onto your printing paper.

Brush a layer of rice paste to the back of the collage paper.

Through a piece of tissue paper, apply pressure using a bone.

The completed collage is flat and ready to overprint when dry.

The linocut has been inked and hand printed over the top.

PROJECT

THE DRY METHOD

This method of *chine-collé* work is my preference. It is not as messy and allows for a neater, cleaner, more precise collage. In this demonstration we will be using an etching press to bond the collage paper directly to the heavy weight backing paper. We will be working with a monoprint matrix as our printed impression; this will require a piece of plastic with a monoprint drawing created on it, similar to the works in Chapter 3. This method will include some preparation and drying time regarding the collage paper, so make sure your papers are dry before commencing your monoprint drawing. The principle is that the collage paper is coated with a thin layer of rice glue. This is left to dry. When ready to collage, the dry glue coated paper is cut into shape and the glue is re-activated when it is in contact with the damp backing paper under the printing press. The printing paper has enough moisture to activate the dried rice glue and thus bond it to the paper. Unlike the wet method, you are working with dry sheets of collage paper and thus it is far easier to cut specific forms and position them – nothing gets covered in wet glue. The use of a high-pressured press creates a beautifully seamless transition from printing paper to collage paper, which is quite stunning.

Start with gravy thick rice glue, paper and a clean brush.

Coat the back of the collage papers in an even layer of glue.

Check in the light for any lumps of rice glue or unevenness.

When the papers are bone dry, create your monoprint matrix.

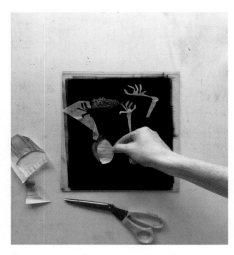

Place cut-out collage papers, glue side up, onto the matrix.

Check all pieces before printing, making sure the glue is up.

Place damp paper in position on the matrix ready for printing.

The pull shows how the collage paper has seamlessly bonded.

The completed impression is set alight by the use of collage.

ADDITIONAL METHODS

Glues

The *chine-collé* methods using nori are very successful, especially the dry method. If you are organized, then you can take time to prepare a stockpile of ready-to-go, glue-coated collage papers that can be cut and bonded when needed. The wet method risks cockling the printing paper, unless you are able to immediately store the print flat, which can cause problems if trying to print and be spontaneous. If you do not have access to a press, but you are wishing to collage directly, then I suggest switching to a non-toxic glue stick, which is brilliant at sticking paper to paper. This way you can be assured that the paper will not buckle. Some artists will use an acrylic medium, PVA or specialist collage glues. But these are all wet glues and when working with paper on paper can cause wrinkling issues. Some artists use spray glues. They can be effective, but they will need to be used in a fully ventilated area and you will need to wear protective breathing equipment. Pre-stretching your impression paper is really the only way to make sure your paper dries flat if working with wet glues.

Making Rice Paste Glue

This process is surprisingly easy and although traditionally rice grains would have been processed and used, for ease we will be using rice flour. It can be bought in most supermarkets these days and is very cheap. You will also need a clean mixing jug, a sterilized jam jar or similar clean storage vessel, and access to water and a stove. Your finished glue will keep in the fridge for up to a week. It can also be frozen in small batches and defrosted when required.

Printing on 9 gms Paper

Some methods of collage work amazingly well if printed upon super lightweight, almost transparent paper. These transparent papers can be printed as you would a heavyweight paper, even with intaglio methods. The papers are left to dry completely and then positioned onto your printed impression, allowing you to mix techniques and textures freely. You need to make sure that you do use a high-quality Japanese paper that is light, yet strong, preferably one made of kozo. When dealing with the exceptionally lightweight paper, the idea of pasting directly with stick glue or even the methods of *chine-collé* just risks damaging the paper too much; it may become unworkable as it gets damp. The method outlined here is very useful and it allows you to paste on thin layers of collage so that they are precisely positioned and become seamless with the backing paper.

Before pasting the paper onto your backing impression, you will need to print an image onto the 9 gms paper. All methods that are printed onto dry paper work exactly as you would if you were printing onto heavier weight paper. Just be more careful when peeling the paper off the matrix. If printing onto the 9 gms paper using a method that requires damp paper, such as a dry-point, then there is a way to do this without having to wet the lightweight paper. When you are ready to print,

Mix 2tbsp of rice flour with 3.5tbsp of water until smooth.

Slowly add 150ml of hot water whilst stirring continuously.

Bring to a simmer and stir continuously until clear and smooth.

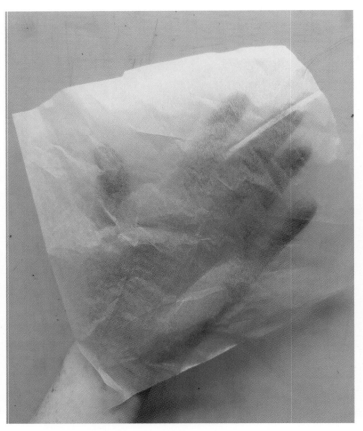

The lightweight Japanese papers are exceptionally strong despite their thinness.

Dung Beetle in Argo, Mary Dalton. This print is primarily a reduction linocut; however, the monochrome beetles in the centre are a stone lithograph printed onto 9 gms Japanese paper. This was bonded and positioned onto the backing impression, giving a clean and crisp outcome.

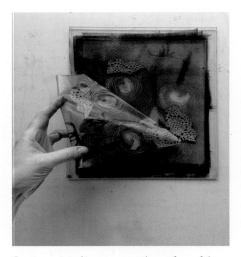

Create a printed image upon the surface of the 9 gms paper.

The completed printed impression on the 9 gms paper must dry.

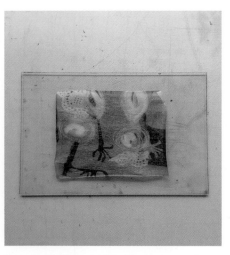

Once dry, lay the print ink side down on a clean Perspex sheet.

lay the inked matrix on the press bed with the dry Japanese paper on top and finally place a piece of damp, clean cartridge paper on top. Blankets go down and then run through the press. The moisture from the cartridge paper will seep through to the 9 gms paper enabling the dry-point to be printed with all details. Peel the 9 gms paper away very carefully from the matrix.

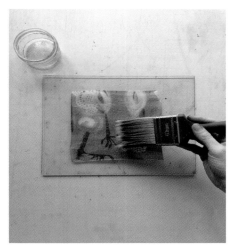

Brush the back with an even layer of gravy thick rice glue. Very carefully peel this coated paper away and place glue side up onto a further clean Perspex sheet.

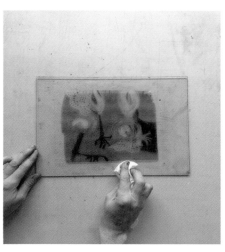

Use a damp cloth to wipe away any loose glue from the edges.

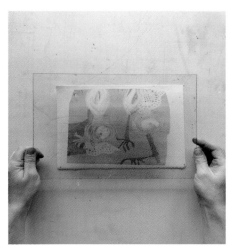

Turn all over and position the print over your backing paper.

Place the Perspex down and rub firmly on the back using your hands.

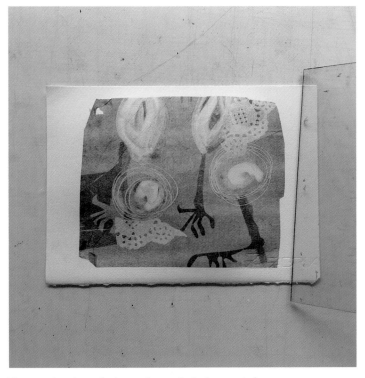

The completed transfer is seamless and crisply executed.

MAKING YOUR OWN COLOURED COLLAGE PAPER

It can be really good fun to print your own stock of collage papers. Additionally, you can tailor them to your own specific colourway or textures, which makes them distinctive and unique. It does require a stretch of uninterrupted time in order to get into the rhythm of the printing, as well as a good selection of coloured inks. You will need a standard inking area set up with roller and inks ready to go. The sheet of plastic will be used to create a solid area of background colour. There will be a drying period between printing background solids and the pattern on top, but the papers can be stacked with tissue paper in between if you are short of hanging space. For this project, I would suggest using an Asian paper with a smooth surface around the 40 gms weight, for instance Kitakata 35 gms, Iwami Natural 30 gms or Kawanaka 29 gms. All of these papers have the strength to receive a large surface area of oil-based ink as well as subsequent patterned layers. They are also lightweight enough to act in a *chine-collé* fashion as well as a basic stick glue collage.

Several colours of backing sheets can be printed for variety.

Roll out a solid colour onto a big Perspex sheet and print.

Offcuts of lino make great abstract collage paper patterns.

Print and overprint the matrices, building up a strong pattern.

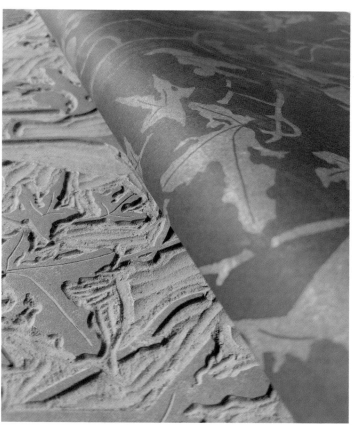
Contrasting backing colour and pattern colour is effective.

Complex abstract patterns form through repeated overprinting.

Using alternative materials can create interesting textures.

Combining traditional and alternative print matrices is fun.

Play with layouts of textures on the press bed for interest.

A full range of interesting and fun papers can be generated.

OILED PAPER COLLAGE

Oiling paper strengthens it and makes it water resistant. By oiling thick paper you are able to create a surface into which intricate designs may be cut and then subsequently printed as a relief surface. Cutting a stencil from oiled paper or card was a traditional way to apply a pattern to Kimono fabric in Japan. These stencils were intricately cut and designed to repeat across the fabric. They are quite stunning in themselves, and old ones often come upon auction sites. The oiled card serves as a great way to make a pattern for collage papers. Instead of applying ink/paste through the gaps cut away and onto the substrate, we ink up the card itself and print this. It allows you to cut detailed patterns with a scalpel that can be printed and re-used. The oil treatment allows a clean and crisp cut which will not fur at the edges. It is a further approach to producing patterned collage papers. You can buy oiled card or paper from all good art stockists. It is usually referred to as oiled Manilla board or oiled stencil card. You can also make your own by coating card with linseed oil and letting it completely dry for a few days.

After it has been printed the first time, you can leave the roll-up ink on the surface to dry, which acts as an additional

You will need thick paper, linseed oil and a clean cotton rag.

Gently rub small circles of oil into the paper's surface.

The paper will become mildly transparent when properly coated.

sealant. For subsequent uses, just a lightly oiled rag wiped gently over the surface should remove the worst of the ink; then it is ready to dry and re-use.

INTRODUCING COLLAGE WITH A HYBRID PRINT

Collage lends itself to be used in a mixed-media unique print, especially if you print your own. Here we are going to look at a large-scale hybrid print, which combines collage, monoprint, stamping, linocut, pencil drawing and various other techniques. The collage papers used in this work are all hand made.

A linocut was hand stamped directly onto the impression paper with bright pink ink. Masks were used to protect non-image areas. Areas of direct stamping were introduced with collage throughout the work. The order in which the lino was introduced was free form, and could be before or after introducing collage. This lack of pre-planning keeps the image fresh.

Fight for the Ivy III, Mary Dalton. This work is 70 × 100cm and composed of hand-printed collage, direct printing and hand drawing. It was worked under a press and by hand.

The pink section was printed directly with lino.

The sections of small, stick-like collage were stuck on with a stick glue because they were quite fiddly. The background orange collage was attached using *chine-collé* under a press. All the collage papers seen here were hand printed. The orange is printed using inked up ferns and using them as masks, arranging freely upon the paper and building layers. The blue was created by overprinting a dark blue solid with a very heavy pale blue top layer. The top layer had squiggles removed, similar to the techniques discussed in Chapter 3.

The pink wood grain section was created using the end of a piece of firewood, inked heavily with pink ink and hand stamped onto the paper. The blue collage paper to the right was made using a linocut, and the black section was created using a printing roller to apply thick black ink directly to the impression paper. Non-image areas were securely masked off.

This little black figure was a linocut hand printed onto very thin Japanese paper and stuck onto the backing paper using the technique discussed in this chapter. It has a beautiful overlay with neighbouring sections and is very flat against the backing paper.

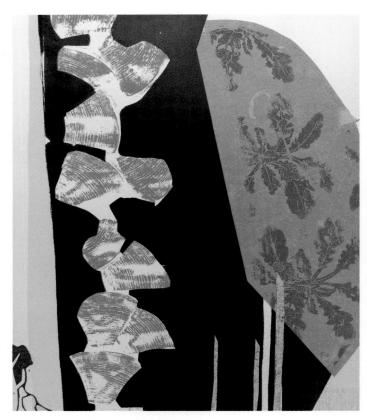

Hand stamping offers some wonderful textural effects.

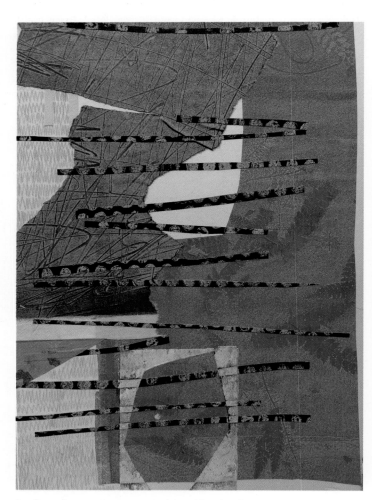

Smaller collage sections were stuck on with a dry glue.

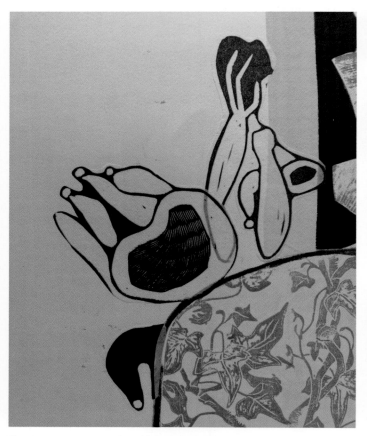

Thin Japanese paper can bond fully with the backing paper.

Building a hybrid collage and printed work can allow the artist to sketch out and think through ideas. Stamps and off-cuts come into use as the mind works through ideas.

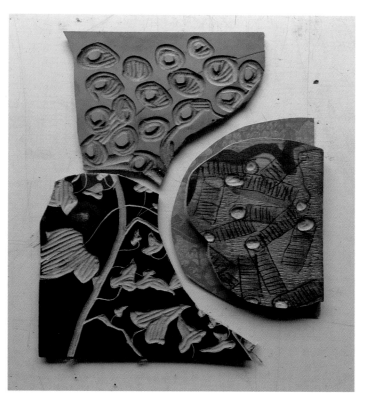

It is important to have a play with arrangements of different matrices.

A student building up a collage print using a nail stamp. It can be fun and expressive.

WHERE TO TAKE COLLAGE

The actual process of collage, when used in conjunction with print, can be clearly seen as a useful and versatile means of expression. But if we look at the process of collaging, then we can apply the process to how we approach a print itself. Collage can teach the artist much about loosening up and applying a free-form technique to liven up a static practice. When working with mixed media prints, try a collage approach to the layout of the matrices. Take a pair of scissors to the lino, a coping saw to the Mokulito or a finger to tear the dry-point card. Have a go at laying the pieces out as if they are a collage to envision how the prints will work when the impression is created. By placing and positioning and repositioning, we often find combinations of effects that would otherwise not be seen.

If working in this manner, then some technical issues of registration will come up as you have different matrices in different positions. Registration possibilities for this are covered in Chapter 10 and are all very manageable. It is about having fun with collage, and bringing this sense of fun and discovery over into the printmaking.

CHAPTER 8

INKS AND COLOUR EFFECTS

Printing inks come in an array of luscious colours to tempt the artist. They are vivid, glossy, inky and spectacular. They have a strength that is second to none and they can be used to produce a multitude of varying effects. In this chapter we will look at oil-based printing inks and how we can utilize rollers, dollies and other methods to create some stunning effects with coloured ink. These techniques can be applied to the various printing methods discussed in this book thus far, and it is with a dextrous mind and an imaginative flair that you can fully utilize the coloured inks. We will explore a few specific follow-along projects, but we will be mainly looking at a multitude of techniques that require you to delve into the inks unhindered by colour theory anxiety.

WHAT IS A COLOURED PRINTING INK?

This may seem a simple question, but as we have learnt in our first chapter, printing ink is very different from paint; it therefore follows that coloured printing ink is also very different from coloured paints. The principle for making the ink is the same: a pigment is ground with a binder to form a product. The binder in the case of traditional oil-based ink is linseed oil. Depending on the coloured pigment used, the grinding process of the ink will be different, and the viscosity of the ink is controlled by using various amounts of different textured oils. Thus we have a glorious, tacky, coloured printing ink. The colour printed on an impression mostly stays true to colour from the tub. You can buy specific pre-mixed colours, such as Rose Pink, or you can buy the basic inks and mix Rose Pink yourself. The latter is far more fun in my mind, and over the years, I have found it to be considerably more economical.

Oil-based printing ink comes in tubes, cartridges and tins.

Extender

Extender, sometimes referred to as transparent base, is an ink additive that is widely used in many print techniques, particularly in relief work such as lino or woodcut. It acts as a transparent base which you tint with a neat colour. Therefore you are able to control the transparency of the ink you are working with. It allows the artist to create the most ephemeral tints, which can be built up in layers, each layer subsequently affecting the next.

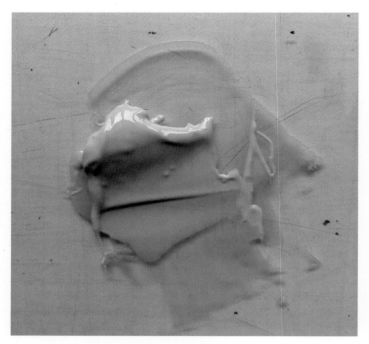

Extender is a transparent printing ink medium.

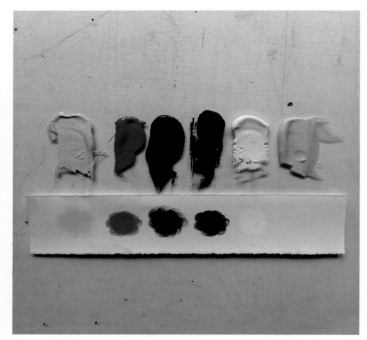

Your basic palette of primaries depends upon artistic preference.

Extender does not make the colour chalky, which is hugely bene-ficial in multi-layered colour work. Colours mixed with extender stay true to the ink you are using to tint. You are not attempting to mix a 'paler' colour, but one that is a true representation of your tinting colour, just in various degrees of transparency.

Ink Additives

There are many ink additives available to the artist beyond extender – French chalk, tack-reducing medium, copper plate oils, dryers, to name a few. They each have a use and indeed many have a specific purpose. You can, however, achieve many phenomenal results without them and they are not essential to still produce high-quality, dynamic colour work. We will look at some of the uses of these additives as and when required in the chapter. (Some are not needed at all; a huge range of techniques can be covered without exploring all the additives.)

Materials

- Inks

  This chapter is about exploring and experimenting with coloured printing inks. We will apply some techniques to print matrices that you may have from previous projects, but we will also learn much without the need to ink up a matrix. You will, however, need coloured printing inks. As with all of the projects and demonstrations in this book, those in this chapter used oil-based inks. The range of colours in oil-based inks is vast and every printmaker is different in their choice of essential colours. Many will form a palette that suits their aesthetic and have a few particular favourite colours and suppliers. To make a start, it is always wise to purchase the primary colours and extender: yellow, red, blue, black, white. In printmaking, if you see the term 'process yellow' this basically means it is the most near to a primary yellow you will find, without a hint of another colour base. The more you explore colour, the more you will find favourites of each of the primaries. For instance, I use a huge amount of primrose yellow in my ink mixing, but very little cadmium yellow. I also use a huge amount of cyan, a throwback from days working on a few CMYK (Cyan, Magenta, Yellow, Black) separation prints. It is a matter of personal preference. Start by exploring the true primaries and expand from these.

- Paper

  You will need a selection of your preferred printing paper. The tonal value of the paper will affect the colours printed on top. In this chapter, we will be working on Fabriano Ecological paper. It is a recycled paper with a clean white pulp, so it will demonstrate clear colour work.

- Basic print set-up

  There are a few follow-along projects which require a press and as much space as you can give for inking.

- Rollers and palette knives
- Plastic monoprint surface
- Linseed oil

  This is for viscosity printing. You can also use thin copper plate ink reducing oil, which is a processed linseed oil.

- Masking tape
- Printing press

TARTAN EXTENDER PRINTING

This is a fun and engaging project to allow some playing with extender printing. You will need to cut your paper to a size that is smaller than your plastic monoprint sheet. You will end up with a dynamic print built up of many layers, allowing you to explore the overlay of ink with extender. It can end up with many layers, so it is advisable to document the layering through notes or photography as you print.

Ideally, you should allow the layers to dry before overprinting with the next. This will give you the most accurate assessment of colour overlay. You can print onto wet ink, but the latest layer may risk pulling up ink from the under layer and not making a clean print. Try not to worry about colour theory and 'correct' colour combinations; enjoy and explore the colours that give you joy. Printing ink is best learnt about when it is out of the tub.

The Challenges with Extender

Extender is very different to roll out than standard oil-based printing ink; it therefore has a few particular difficulties that occur. One of the most common is that it rolls up stringy and gloopy and makes the sound of a thick, wet hiss. Basically, too

Choose a selection of ink colours and extender to print with.

Mix three extended colours and evenly roll up the palest ink.

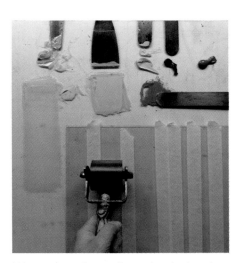

Using tape, mask out strips on the plastic and ink up a few.

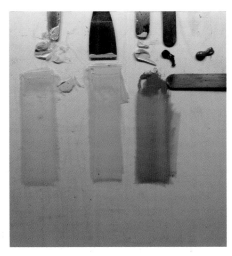

Roll out the remaining colour mixes and ink up more strips.

Peel away the masking tapes before printing under the press.

Carefully peel away the print revealing the first impression.

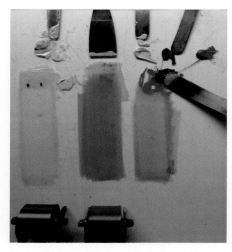

Change the tint of the extended mixes with drops of neat ink.

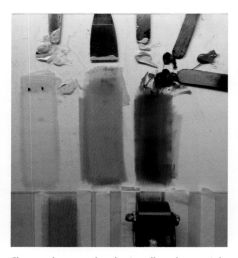

Clean and re-tape the plastic, roll up the new ink as before.

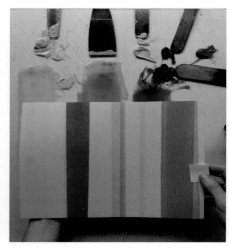

Print the new striped matrix on top of the first impression.

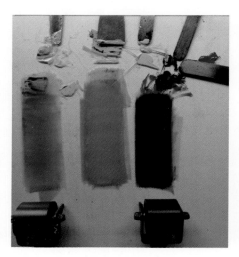

Tint the colours further and repeat the previous print steps.

Print the impression at a different angle, allowing cross-over.

The print showing extended inks overlaying to create new colour.

A roll-up that is too thick and gloopy.

A roll-up that is the right consistency.

A dirty roller can affect the roll-up.

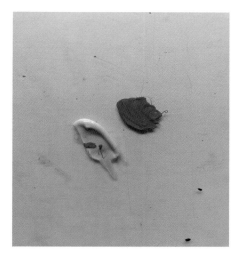
Always add drops of colour to the extender to tint, not extender to the colour.

Use clean tissue to pat off excess ink.

The clear result of removing excess ink.

much ink has been laid out on the surface. There is a tendency to add more extender-based ink upon the roll-up surface because it is tricky to see the colour you have created when rolling out. You actually need a similar amount to standard ink, perhaps marginally less, to compensate for the tackiness. If the stringy, hissy roll-up occurs, scrape some off, and roll up until a nice even hiss is heard.

Extender is hugely sensitive to tinting. If your roller, palette knife, roll-up surface, print matrix or anything else is not clean, the extender will pick this up and the colour will be affected. Make sure everything is spotless before you start.

When tinting extender, it is always advisable to add drops of the neat colour to the extender, not the extender to the colour. If you do the former, then you have control of the depth of colour being created. You can always add more of your neat colour to the extender, but you cannot take it away.

Extender takes significantly longer to dry than standard inks. You can add chemical dryers to the ink to speed up drying time, or you can just be patient. If you end up printing a really thick layer of extender and it looks gloopy, you can take a clean piece of tissue paper to the surface of the wet impression, gently pat the back to pick up excess ink and peel away the tissue paper.

FURTHER EXTENDER POSSIBILITIES

Opaque White and Extender

As we have learnt, extender is a great medium for layering up transparencies. It also increases the gloss of a print and can make it look rather luxurious! Extender is mainly used in relief work or in any technique that uses a roller to apply the ink layer. Extender has a completely different effect to a colour than opaque white.

Poppy red ink in the middle, with 50 per cent extender to the left, and 50 per cent opaque white to the right.

Purple ink in the middle, with 50 per cent extender to the left, and 50 per cent opaque white to the right.

Neat opaque white used in this print by Mary Dalton to knock back the background layers prior to further printing.

Extender will keep the tint true to its original colour, whereas opaque white will make it chalkier and flatter.

The differences between the two can be used to the advantage of the printmaker if used wisely and imaginatively. Sometimes, opaque white can even be added in a middle layer to a print to obliterate the under layers, allowing the artist to rebuild new fresh colours on top of this section.

Extender as Glue

This is one extremely fun use of extender. The tackiness of the ink created by the extender can be utilized as a glue layer on a printed impression. For instance, imagine printing the last layer on a reduction linocut with nothing but extender. Assuming all other ink layers are bone dry, once the impression is pulled and the extender still wet, you can sprinkle the layer with glitter, pigment, flocking – anything that is a fine enough powder to stick to the extender layer. Once completely dry, the excess is blown off, leaving the amazing, decorated layer only where the extender sat. Traditional flocked wallpaper used wet ink/glue as a surface for the flocking to adhere to, so this technique is not completely mad. Do test before applying to your unique print though. Some of the pigments, such as the metallic ones, may also marginally adhere to other areas of the print, but generally speaking it is very effective and fun. You will also need to roll your extender ink out slightly thicker than usual to give more adhesive power.

Printing a sample linocut with a tinted yellow extended ink.

Sprinkling on non-toxic green pigment onto the wet lino ink.

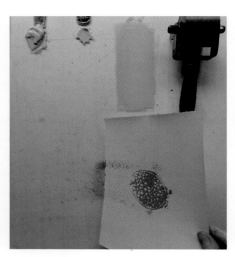

Tapping off excess pigment so it only sticks to the wet ink.

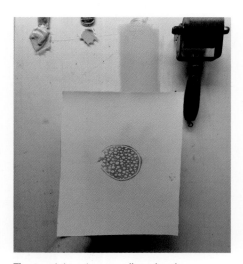

The remaining pigment adhered to the wet extended ink only.

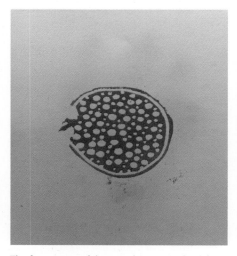

The fun texture of the raised pigment clearly seen up close.

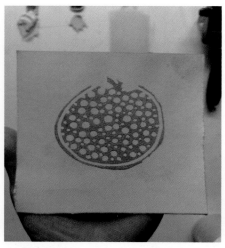

Metallic pigments work very well using extended ink as glue.

INK MIXING TECHNIQUE

Mixing printing ink is slightly different to mixing paint. There are some basic techniques that will allow you to be more effective in your process. By staying neater, cleaner and more efficient, it leaves more time, with less stress, to actually print.

Keeping Colours Clean

If you are utilizing a lot of colour work in printing, it can be beneficial to keep colours clean and separate from each other. For instance, if you are printing with red and green at the same time, the two areas should be kept separate, since any contamination on either part will cause for a muddy effect on the ink. This will obviously require more equipment and space, so is not always practical, but it is worth learning from and pursuing.

If you are using one roller and minimal equipment, then you can just clean down in between each new colour. The other method is to be a little more free-form and, instead of mixing brand new colours, add ink directly to the roll-up surface, use the roller to blend the new colour in, and work from there. This is quite a fun and dynamic approach, but you will always be working within the same colour range, since it would be difficult to dramatically alter the colour since each colour is affecting the next.

Squeeze ink gently from the bottom of metal tubes.

Scraping ink across the top surface from ink tubs.

Using a squeeze gun to force ink from a cartridge.

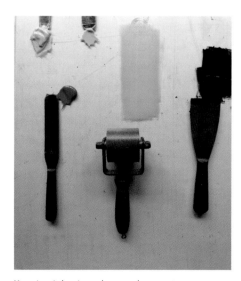

Keeping ink mixes clean and separate ensures clean roll-ups.

Use the side of a palette knife to scrape up all the ink mix.

Place ink in the same spot, use the tip to mix back and forth.

Repeat the scraping and mixing steps until the ink is mixed.

Use the edge of a wide, flat palette knife to scrape up ink.

Force the ink out flat with the edge and scrape and repeat.

A rolled-out primrose yellow ink ready for colour changing.

Using a palette knife to add red spots into the yellow ink.

Using a roller to 'mix' together the red and the yellow ink.

The completed orange ink after the red and yellow are mixed.

Storing Colours

Oil-based inks, if no driers have been added, can store all day and even overnight without drying out. If you have mixed a colour you really like and have much of it left, scrape it up and place it upon a stiff piece of card such as a cereal packet scrap. Then, cover this neatly with some aluminium foil to prevent air getting to it. Using your fingers, gently work around the blob of ink so that the foil sits tightly to the edges, thus removing as much air as possible. When ready to use, take the foil off, scrape up any ink and place on your roll-up area ready for use.

Colour Matching

Colour matching is an art in itself, and a highly experienced printmaker can mix a colour accurate to even the smallest sample given to them. When learning and you wish to keep a sample of a mixed colour for future reference, there are some pointers to help you match it again. The key is to use a system that works for you and stick with it. Like registration, do not change the system you have designed halfway through, as it will confuse matters. The most common technique is to refer to beads of ink as a way to describe proportions of each colour used in a mix. The bead can then be adjusted up or down depending on

Sealing the edges of a foil ink package to keep the air out.

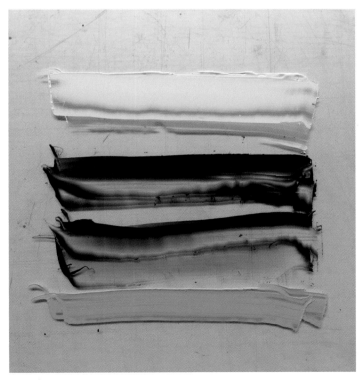

Beads of ink laid out.

the amount of ink you will be mixing. It is all based on proportions (for example, 1 bead of Poppy Red, 2 beads Cyan Blue, 0.5 beads of Primrose Yellow). If this is noted and stored, when you come to mix the colour again, it will be accurate. Like a cooking recipe, you can increase the volume or decrease it according to requirements. This means that you will need to take notes of the colours added as you mix the first batch.

Commercially, many printing inks are weighed to exact proportions so that the mix is spot on each time. When working on a fine art system, the colour mixing can be a bit more free-form, and so sometimes even the bead system does not work, in which case it is down to taking notes as you go, such as 'a drop of cyan,' 'two drops of rose pink.' Then when you come to mixing a new batch, you have a general guide to follow, but you will also need to adjust marginally as you go to ensure an accurate colour match.

ROLLER EFFECTS

The printmaking roller is like a paintbrush. It can be used to apply all manner of wonderful colour ink effects to a print matrix. The most used is probably the blend, which describes when two or more colours are rolled out with the one roller, creating an *ombré* effect across the roller's surface. This is quite stunning, and also introduces some seriously amazing layering options for the artist. There are also many roller effects that are a one-off, and can only be applied a few times before they all merge together. This style suits unique prints and generates some very unusual effects. Embrace the printmaking roller and have fun with the options it can give you.

Blends

The printmaking blend is a hugely satisfying technique to learn and develop. It works well with all rollers: the wider your roller, the more colour options you have in introducing to your blend. Blends can be editioned; you need to stay attentive to the roll-up surface and refreshing your ink levels. There are one or two tricks when learning about blends that will entail confident and professional practice further down the line.

The use of a guide marked onto the roll-up surface is very useful when learning about keeping the blend line. The blend line describes the line where different coloured inks meet and merge. The artist has the option of how wide this blend line is by overlapping the bead of ink applied or by moving the roller from side to side as you roll up to increase the width of the blend line. As you have blends of more complex colour numbers, then you will need to stay very tight on your rolling up to make sure that the blend lines do not end up mixing together, to keep all

Using a palette knife to apply beads of the first ink colour.

The second colour applied not quite overlapping the first one.

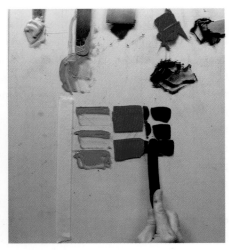

The final third colour laid down, not overlapping the second.

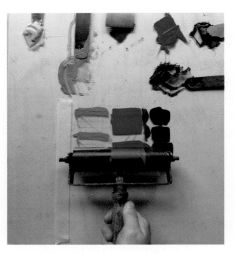

Rolling out the blend, keeping the edge in line with the tape.

An evenly rolled out blend on both roller and roll-up surface.

A test piece of plain dry-point card inked up with the blend.

The printed blend on paper, showing the even inking and colour.

Complex roller blends are hugely versatile in printmaking.

The blend on this print goes from a fluorescent, bright pink to a deep brown.

the unique colours clean. The more you practise blends, the less likely you will need the guidelines on your roll-up surface.

If you are producing an edition with a blend, you will need to keep an eye on both the blend line on the roll-up surface and the blend line on the matrix. The more the roller is used, the more chance the blend line has of widening and altering both colours either side. Never be afraid of completely cleaning up and starting a blend again if you feel this is happening. If planning to produce a large edition, make sure you have enough ink pre-mixed to allow for frequent cleaning and fresh roll-ups.

Blends can be as subtle or as bold as the artist wishes. They can be used for a single layer print, a roll-over, or in a multi-layered print. They are truly brilliant and something that is quite unique to printmaking.

Unique Roller Approaches

If pursuing unique printmaking, then you will find you have a scrumptious array of one-of-a-kind roller effects to utilize. The key is to experiment and be bold with the colours used. Every time you roll the roller out, it is subtly mixing the inks on your surface and your matrix. To stand a greater chance of some unique roller effects working, you should aim to work with more contrasting colours, so that the blending effect is less visually apparent. You also need to bear in mind the width of your roller. The edges of the roller will impact the roll-up on the matrix and generate thin lines, or tram lines, across the plate. If possible, choose a roller wider than your matrix, or embrace and work with these edges.

A roller being used to carefully roll up the unique effect.

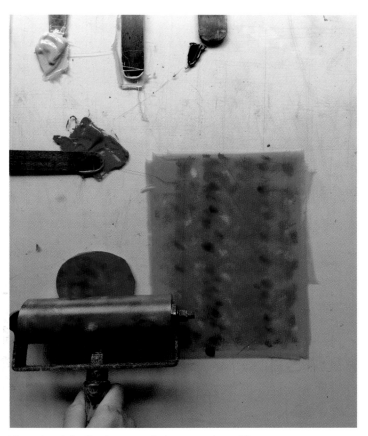

The unique ink effect being applied to a test piece of lino.

Multi-coloured contrasting ink dots added to a clean roll-up.

The character of the unique ink effect showing in the print.

VISCOSITY PRINTING

Viscosity printing describes colour work that involves changing the oiliness of the printing ink. By changing the oiliness, or viscosity, of the ink, you are able to layer multiple colour roll-ups on the same print matrix without them affecting one another. This can then be printed in a single pull. For instance, I ink up a plastic monoprint surface in a solid red rectangle. I then mix up a blue ink with a drop or two of extra

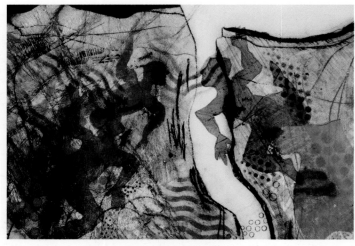

Across the Water, Ruth Barrett-Danes. A beautiful example of colour and monochrome ink work executed using paper dry-point by Ruth Barrett-Danes. Note the wonderful layers of darker tones in the figure on the right underneath the orange, adding depth to the work.

linseed oil, altering the viscosity of the ink. I then wipe away an abstract circle from the red monoprint surface and roll over the entire surface with the blue ink. The background will be a clean purple and the wiped away circle will be blue. The blue ink has a different viscosity to the red ink due to the extra oil added. Thus, when the blue is rolled over the top of the red, the red does not peel off and mix with the blue ink; in fact you have two layers of ink sitting atop of one another, layering beautifully. If you continue to change the viscosity of your inks, then you can continue to build up the roll-overs with the use of the masks to create a very complex image printed in a single pull.

PROJECT

VISCOSITY ABSTRACT

This project is aimed at allowing you to freely explore the possibilities of viscosity printing, whilst also getting used to changing the texture of the inks. You will need a range of coloured inks, a roller, a printing press, and inking set-up. You will also need linseed oil to alter the viscosity of the oil-based inks. We will be using the sheet of plastic as a monoprint surface and also some scraps of dry-point card.

Roll up a thin base layer of extended colour onto a plastic.

Use masks and previously used techniques to remove some ink.

Use linseed oil to change the viscosity of the next colour.

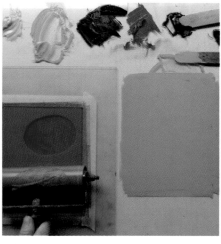

Roll out the second colour once only to avoid repeat images.

Have a play with unique effects for the third viscosity roll.

Using masks and mark-making techniques to remove further ink.

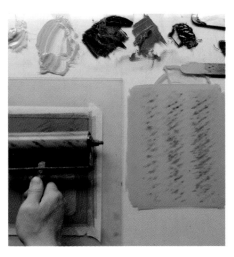

Roll over again, trying not to disrupt the unique roller effect.

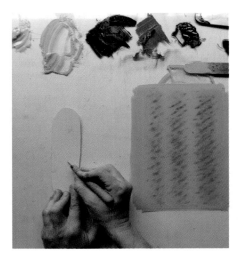

Mark-making dry-point card to use as an additional element.

The card can be inked and rolled over using dynamic colours.

The plastic with tape off and card placed on, ready to print.

The single pull of the viscosity print revealing the layers.

The completed viscosity print illustrating the cleanliness of the colours. The layers of the green and pink coming through where masks were used are classic viscosity printing, keeping colours and layers clean.

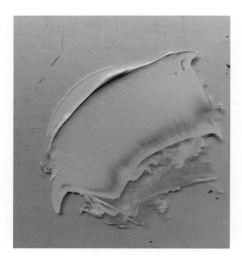

Opaque white is often loved or loathed by printmakers.

Opaque white added to lime green (bottom) changing the tone and adding a distinct flatness.

A linocut inked with opaque white printing on top of pink.

OPAQUE WHITE

Opaque white, like extender, is a very powerful ink to use in works. In can be mixed with other colours to make them flatter and chalkier, but it can also be used at any point during a multi-layered print to add a complete change of atmosphere, and in some cases, completely obliterate previous layers. White will come in various types, from titanium to chalk white, and many in between. In my personal practice, I tend to use a very basic general all-purpose, non-toxic opaque white. I avoid the titanium or lead whites, especially when grinding my own ink, as the powders need a professional ventilation set-up. Opaque white can be quite a stiff ink, so it may need a drop of oil and some working to loosen it.

Opaque White as a Mixer

Opaque white has the awesome effect of making inks appear flatter, or heavier. It will also make the colour significantly chalkier. But this is something that is very useful in colour print work, particularly in relief work when in contrast with a cleaner, more vivid colour made with extender. In some cases, a drop of opaque white is just what is needed to give a colour an extra zing. For instance, when making a light lime green the opaque white will bring through the yellow base to the green, making it visually more vibrant.

An opaque white ink mix added to a complex layered print can really bring it to life and ground the image. The contrast between the opaque white mix and the other layers is quite special and one that can be used to great effect. This mainly

Opaque white overprinting to knock back the background layer.

through to the darkest, but why do this when it is far more fun to shake it up? This technique works very well in reduction or layered relief work where the ink layer is thick. The opaque white will provide a strong backdrop to rebuild a whole new area of contrasting colour without the previous colour layers influencing it.

INK, BUT NOT QUITE

It is worth bringing into this chapter a few alternative approaches to adding colour in printmaking that do not involve using ink. The most common is hand colouring after the print is dry, and there are a few more we will look at that are more unconventional but quite distinctive. They all have their uses and specific applications that are worth exploring when approaching colour work in a specific print.

refers to relief work, since the thickness and flatness of the opaque white ink means it will sit proudly atop the previous layers. However, opaque white can also be used in intaglio work, such as paper dry-point, to directly ink up the plate. You will need to print over a darker ink colour to see your lines, but as long as the previous darker layer is bone dry, you should see some beautiful effects.

The final trick of opaque white (I say final, but I am sure there are many more) is to obliterate all under-layer information, effectively giving the artist a blank canvas to rebuild layers. In more classic printmaking, you work from the lightest colours

Hand Colouring

Hand colouring is just that: colouring a print by hand after the printed impression is dry. It has been used for centuries and traditionally watercolour is used to apply the colour. If using oil-based ink, the watercolour will resist the oil-based impression and seep beautifully into the non-image areas of your print. Before using watercolour, you will need to stretch your printed impression so that the paper does not buckle or warp with the wet watercolour. This is covered in Chapter 10. Once the hand colouring has been completed, the print can be carefully cut away from the board using a craft knife and trimmed.

You can also hand colour a print with any other medium you wish – pencils, wax crayons, felt tips, pastels. Each one will respond differently to the dry impression, but each allows the artist to apply specific areas of colour to the print. In some cases,

The pre-soaked print ready to be stretched on a board.

Using a damp sponge to wet traditional gum tape.

Applying the gum tape to the edges of the paper, sticking it to the board.

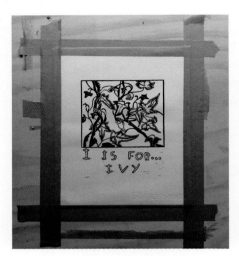

The completed stretched print ready to dry.

Once completely dry, the paper may be hand coloured with watercolour.

Basic wax crayons can be used to alter the texture of an impression.

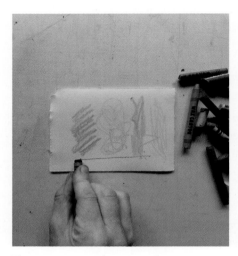

The crayons are used to create a basic underdrawing on the paper.

It is clear to see the beautiful texture change where the wax crayon is.

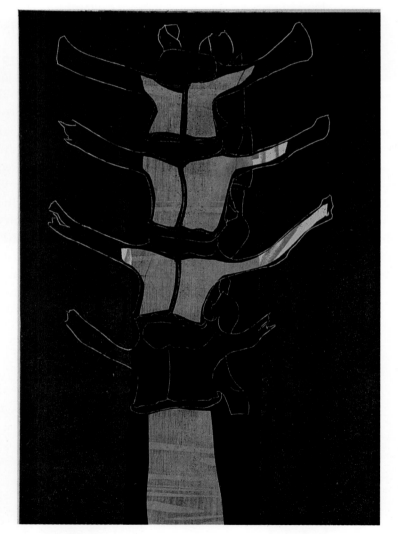

Deer Spine, Mary Dalton. An example of using wax crayon as an underdrawing before printing a monoprint on top. The crayon was used to create the 'squiggle' running either side of the spine. The main grey monoprint was printed as a ghost over the crayon, so the crayon marks were more visible as a darker black.

it is far more efficient and logical to add a tiny area of highlight colour by hand to a print than to prepare a matrix.

Wax Crayons

Wax crayons partially resist oil-based inks, which can offer some subtle effects on an impression. If they are used as an under drawing before an inked impression is added, they create a change in texture of the oil-based ink. Children's wax crayons work very well; by their nature they prevent fine details being added so they force the artist to be very gestural and liberal with the marks they make, which can really open up new possibilities. The thicker the wax crayon marks, the more wax laid down, and thus the stronger the effect when in conjunction with the ink. Here, we are using black ink printed under an etching press and you will be able to see the change in impression texture. If you use extended ink, or thinner layers, or hand print, they all have slightly different effects.

Coloured Pencils and Underdrawing

Using pencils to create a preliminary area of colour prior to adding the printed impression can add a really interesting dynamic and texture to a print. Most coloured pencils are wax-based, and thus also add a marginal level of resistance, which can be fun and unpredictable. The pencil allows you to produce a finer result than the wax crayon, which is very broad, and you can specify exactly where you wish to add the marks. They come in a wonderful array of seductive colours and it is very refreshing to draw directly onto the printing paper rather than print on it, which in essence is more removed from the direct mark-making.

The use of pencils is a great way to add texture and colour to prints prior to adding a top layer. It works particularly well with unique prints because you are not having to worry about how to replicate the effects for an edition. Working with pencils, crayons and other under-drawing processes is a very direct addition to a print, allowing you to feel your way around the work intuitively and expressively.

Wax-based colouring pencils being used to create an underdrawing.

A basic black has been printed over the top with leaf masks added.

A base layer print created with coloured pencils and monoprint.

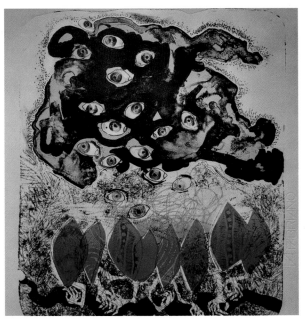
The completed unique print with the top lithographic layer added.

CHAPTER 9

CELEBRATING THE UNIQUE: PRINT BEYOND PAPER

Printmaking is all about paper, right? Not quite. If there is anything we have learnt, it is how to look at printmaking in a different light. But also to see that all printmaking is interconnected through the simple principles of a matrix and an impression. We have been working on papers as our substrate, producing and learning through the creation of an image-based impression. In this chapter, we will be looking at how these paper impressions can be incredibly complex by combining techniques. We will also be dipping our toes into the magical world of print beyond paper. Printmaking that is immersive, sculptural, tactile. There will be one or two projects to play with as a means of an introduction to this innovative world, alongside a look at some specific artwork to really grasp the potentials of print in the future.

STIR IT UP

Mixed technique prints are an art form in themselves, taking a whole new level of printmaking expertise and knowledge to make them successful. Throughout this book we have been exploring them with vigour, combining processes from across chapters to produce expressive, unique prints. These prints can often be referred to as hybrid prints. They take patience and commitment to fully explore, but the possibilities are luscious and inviting. Once individual techniques have been explored, the artist can freely pick and choose which one best suits the expression required for the work in hand and begin to see which combine well technically and aesthetically. Hybrid prints truly celebrate what it is to print. They become expressions of the uniqueness of printmaking and celebrate its place in the fine art world.

Creating hybrid prints on paper is complex and challenging, yet hugely fun.

The Bones of a Hybrid

Building up a hybrid print at first seems very complex and it certainly takes a little practice and effort to make sure the impression does not look contrived or over-worked. But that

Breaking Through, Liz Cotgreave. A mixed-media print created during a Hybrid Printmaking course. It shows many layers of various techniques executed with precision and finesse. The yellow area in the centre is a paper dry-point printed near the start, which was built upon with various layers of monoprint and collage.

is only because it is something new that needs to be had fun with. Once the language reaches a conversational level, then it can flow quite easily to allow you to build challenging hybrid prints without losing the spontaneity of expression. This requires the artist to think beyond the conventions of print-making and requires an approach to printmaking that does not always follow the steadfast rules laid out. So all in all, it sounds pretty awesome.

The construction of these prints has no real rules. Any layer can be applied on any other layer, and any technique can be mixed with any other technique. However, there are a few loose guides to have in mind – the main one being that an intaglio print plate gives a cleaner representation of original marks if printed directly onto paper. In essence this means that these matrices with their thinner ink layers struggle to make an impact if overprinted onto layers of previously laid down ink. For instance, a dry-point may not print that clearly on top of a thick reduction linocut, but it would work beautifully as the first layer to the reduction linocut.

Oil-based ink needs time to dry. If you are wishing for a clean impression over the top of a previous layer, then that layer needs to be bone dry. This is essential. If wishing to print wet on wet,

that is, a wet layer of ink on top of another wet layer of ink, then just be aware you may get puckering of the ink and lose some detail.

When working with multiple processes, you will be switching from printing on damp paper to dry throughout the print. If you are wishing for precise registration at any point, you will need to be aware that as paper is soaked the fibres stretch, and as it dries they will contract, causing your paper to shrink. Thus you go to print your next layer on the dry paper and the whole image has shrunk significantly. To help prevent this, if printing on damp paper, as soon as you have finished, stretch the paper following the instructions in Chapter 10 and your paper should not shrink too much. Thus you will be able to continue in register.

Planning the layers and the areas of different techniques should certainly be pondered, but not overthought. By over thinking, the impression will lose its vigour and life and look static and contrived. This is of course easier said than done, as the temptation is to write down all layers and colours and areas in a little sketchbook and meticulously work from this. But try not to. Make a few notes, sure, but also go with the flow. If you are midway through, and the lino layer you had written down is just not working, then do not print it. Find an alternative and follow the actual print as a guide, not the preconceived print in your head.

Hybrid Print Analysis

In order to have a greater understanding of how a hybrid print is conceived and made, we are going to look at two very different hybrid, unique prints. The first is created using only techniques we have looked at in this book. The second uses one technique that is not covered in this book and demonstrates how printmaking can continually evolve and expand. This breakdown will give an understanding of how they were made.

PRINT 1

This print is made up of five different processes: reduction linocut, lithino, monoprint, paper dry-point and *chine-collé*. It is a unique print that was printed over a period of a few weeks to allow for the drying time of the various layers. It has all been hand printed onto a 145 gms Zerkall smooth white paper, apart from the paper dry-point which was printed under a press onto damp paper.

The first layer printed was the yellow urn shape in the background. This was simply done by inking up a thick piece of paper in solid primrose yellow and hand printing it. Once this was dry, a lithino matrix was created. On this matrix was the mono-chrome intestinal shape, which was created using water and stick

Under the Oak Tree, Mary Dalton Print 1 example.

tusche washes, and the wood grain texture on the urn, created using drawing ink and a dip pen. These were etched and inked up in a grey black and a peach on the same matrix. They were hand printed in register on top of the dried yellow urn.

Next to print was the pink to red blend in the background. This was printed as a monoprint. The non-image areas on the impression were carefully masked off with tissue paper and the blend was rolled out on a piece of plastic sheet. This was laid in position and the impression was hand printed.

The next process was another lithino layer on the same piece of lino used previously. The previous marks were sanded off and the lino was drawn up with the spots using neat drawing ink. These were processed and hand printed in cyan.

The lithino matrix was cleaned off and a linocut was carved into it to create the black outline for the grey intestinal shape. This was cut knowing that after this stage, the blue hands would also be carved into the same piece of lino. The black outline was hand printed in register and then the pale blue hand shapes were carved and printed. They were printed with a heavy opaque white base to knock back previous layers. Once hand printed, they were further carved to create the finger shapes and printed in register in the darker blue.

Thus far all the work has been hand printed onto dry paper. Now the paper dry-point is to be printed. The little shapes were cut individually from the top of an old foil cake tin. They were marked, inked up in soft black, wiped back clean and rolled over in a pink peach. Each was placed faced down onto the paper on the press bed, as opposed to paper on top. This was because

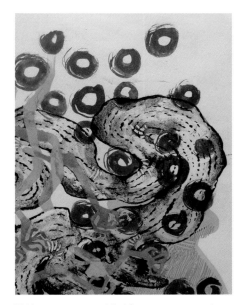

Lithino cyan spots added fun movement and colour to the work.

The monochrome lithino intestine was hand printed.

Lino was carved using traditional tools and printed in black.

Paper dry-point forms were printed as first pulls and ghosts.

A *chine-collé* layer was added, made from hand-printed paper.

I did not wish for an emboss around the dry-point pieces, I wished them to appear flat upon the impression. It also had the secondary benefit that I could place them in exact register. The paper was lightly sponged damp and run through at very high pressure. Areas were masked off to prevent the dry-point printing upon certain areas. The paper was fed back through immediately after the first pull to allow the printing of a few ghosts of the dry-point shapes.

The very final layer, once all inks were dry, was to add a bold section of pre-printed *chine-collé*. This had been printed at a previous date using scrunched up dry-point card inked in dark brown, rolled over lightly in a buff colour and printed with a black background. It was printed on a 39 gms Japanese kozo mix paper. The paper was pre-prepared with homemade rice paste glue and left to dry, allowing a precise shape to be cut. This *chine-collé* was run through the press onto damp paper and bonded beautifully. A complex print finished off with a very simple, bold and graphic process bringing the whole impression together.

PRINT 2

This second print uses a photo lithographic method that we have not covered in this book. In essence, it works exactly like the lithographic methods we have been using thus far – the main difference being that the drawing is exposed to UV light. Anywhere the light penetrates will become a non-image area and everywhere the drawing prevents the light reaching will be your positive drawing. Thus, you can also use materials to create strong silhouettes to block off the exposure to UV light. In this print, I exposed two bracken leaves, allowing me to generate a strong, graphic leaf shape to ink up. All the other techniques are covered in this book. It is interesting to see how the processes have so much relevance to other methods beyond those we have covered.

The print was printed under an etching press and by hand onto Fabriano Rosaspina 220 gms paper in white.

The first layer to be printed was a large piece of dry-point card, with a torn edge. The card was not marked with any tools; instead the focus was on the shape of the element and the distinctive torn edges. The piece was inked up at the edges in a burnt sienna and rolled over in a scummy yellow. It was printed under an etching press onto dry paper to give a more speckled effect. Once this was done, the photo lithographic leaves could be printed. They were inked and printed following the standard litho procedure. It was printed under an etching press onto dry paper and the paper was trapped in the rollers each time to allow the bracken matrix to be re-inked in another green and

Dear Deer with Fadir, Mary Dalton Print 2 example.

Photo lithographic ferns were printed multiple times in green.

Opaque white was used as an underprint to the lino sections.

run through again in perfect register. This process was repeated many times until the leaves had life and soul.

The diagonal stripes, or rain, were printed next, using a second photo litho printing plate and drawn with ink. This could be easily replicated with Mokulito or lithino. They were printed in several colours, including the dark blue blend, trapping the paper and rolling through the press many times.

The next process used was a multi-plate reduction linocut. The beech leaves and the abstract birch tree trunks were all carved from individual pieces of lino that were stuck down onto a backing board. Before any carving took place, the impression paper was taped directly to the backing board in register and the lino was inked up in opaque white and hand printed. This ensured cleaner colours in the subsequent layers. The lino sections were then treated as reduction linocuts and inked up many times in numerous colours to produce the finished result.

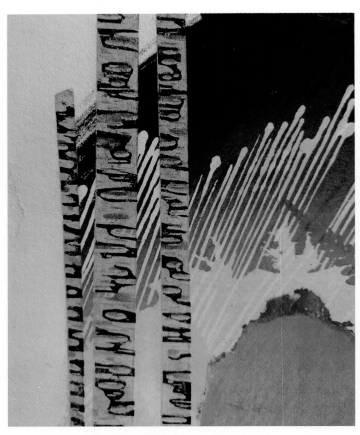

Lino pieces were reduction cuts individually inked and printed.

Mask-making and monoprint process created a change in texture.

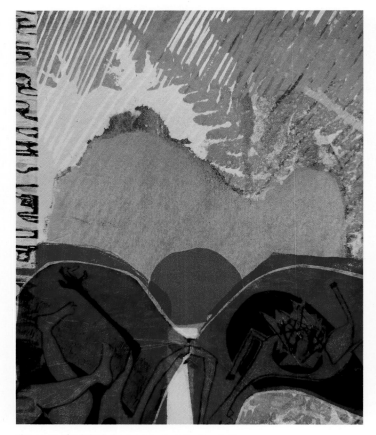

Flat areas of solid ink were printed under the etching press.

Finally, a paper dry-point *chine-collé* section was glued on.

Work now begins on the pink organs on the left of the impression. The backing section of pink squiggles and yellow was created using the monoprint techniques. A piece of plastic was inked up pink, and squiggles removed with a suitable tool. A mask was placed on the impression and the pink section hand printed. Whilst the pink ink was still wet, a piece of paper was torn to shape, inked up in yellow and hand printed over this pink squiggle area. The wet-on-wet effect gave some interesting texture.

The light pink and dark pink shapes of the organs were printed using a similar method of inking up paper shapes. They were printed under the etching press to ensure a very flat and even impression. The details of the figure and textures in the organs were created on a piece of scrap paper dry-point card. It was drawn, inked up in black, rolled over in bright pink and printed onto acid-free tissue paper. This tissue paper was then stuck down onto the impression when the ink was dry. The use of basic tissue paper meant that it had a slightly crumpled look to the *chine-collé* application, which worked well to add texture to the work.

MAKING IT SCULPTURAL

The impressions we have been taking so far in this book have been on paper. The majority of fine art printmaking is done using paper as the substrate. Paper is truly amazing and as we have learnt, comes in many different varieties, each offering a different end aesthetic. But there are some very effective ways to instantly turn an otherwise 2D impression into a 3D sculptural impression. We will look at four main ideas, all of which offer the artist a very efficient way to introduce printmaking into sculpture. There are of course many other approaches, but the techniques we will cover give you a great starting point. Due to the differing nature of each technique, materials will be listed for each project.

PLASTER CAST PRINTMAKING

Artist's casting plaster acts as a brilliant substrate to create an accurate impression of most printed works covered in this book. The plaster when poured on top of an inked matrix will not only pick up the detail of the matrix to a very good standard, but it will also take an impression of the textural surface of the carved marks, incised lines or other relief work. The resultant form is wonderfully interesting and very strong as a piece of relief sculpture. The technique is simple in principle,

A plaster cast print offers the artist a range of printmaking textures upon a three-dimensional surface. You are dealing with flat textures as well as relief work.

but may take a few attempts to get the desired result. It is essential that oil-based ink is used, otherwise the water in the plaster will react with the water in the ink and create a sludgy mess. It is a fine balance between ink and plaster consistency, all of which can be achieved through practice and engagement.

PROJECT

HYBRID PLASTER CAST PRINT

This project is great fun and can whittle away many hours of inky experimentation. You will need to gather a few specialist materials before you start. You have to use traditional linseed oil-based printing ink. It does not work very well with water-based oil washable inks or similar hybrid inks.

Materials

- Plaster of Paris
  You can order specialist varieties of plaster from suppliers, which is brilliant if this technique suits you as you can order up to 25kg bags. If just having a go, then get a small bag (about 5kg) of plaster of Paris from a craft shop.
- Mould
  You will also need a silicone or foil cake mould in the size of your choice. This acts as a great recyclable and even re-usable ready prepared mould. You will not need a release agent.
- Protective equipment
  You will need a face mask and gloves to mix the plaster, plus a mixing and pouring area suitably protected with old newspaper or dust sheet.
- Mixing equipment
  An old whisk is brilliant to mix. You will need a bucket and an old measuring jug or similar container, and a water supply. When available, I use rainwater to save drinking water.
- Printing matrices
  You will need to gather a small selection of prepared paper dry-point matrices and a couple of lino off-cuts. Treat them as shown in previous chapters to give a range of marks.

- Relief textures
  Find a few interesting relief textures that can be inked and cast. You are looking for flat items with surface texture, for instance, lace, corrugated metal sheeting, model-making perforated metal sheet, scrunched up and flattened tin foil.
- Standard printmaking supplies

After the Plaster has Cured

The plaster relief takes a few days to fully cure, depending upon the thickness. When the relief feels cold to the touch and does not warm up when you place your hand upon it, then it is most likely cured. It will also feel significantly lighter than the first time you removed it from the mould because all the extra moisture has evaporated off. Once the plaster print has cured, you are able to carve, scratch, sand and scrape away at the surface for further effects. Please do always wear a face mask when doing this, so as not to breathe in the loose plaster dust created.

Plaster as the Print Matrix

As well as using plaster as a casting medium, you can carve directly into a plaster tile and treat it as a reduction relief print. It creates some beautifully textured prints. The process is very simple. You first need to cast a solid slab of plaster the size of your intended print. It needs to be left to completely cure, which can take up to a week. When bone dry you can then carve into it using relief

All the matrices that you are using need to be inked up and prepared following the guidance in previous chapters. You can then start laying them out in the mould, ink facing up.

Build up the layer in the mould, including inked up relief textures. Make sure there is nothing too small or light, because this risks floating up in the liquid plaster and getting submerged.

Include bold linocuts and layer with confidence. Dry-point works best at the bottom of the mould, and lino can be layered up. The more layering, the more risk there is the plaster will seep underneath the layers and lift them up. A balance is found through experimentation.

Mix your plaster marginally thicker than the guideline on the container. Do not mix with your hands; use a whisk or spare tool. It needs to be like cake batter. This allows you to place small preliminary amounts on some layers to hold them in place before you pour the larger amount of plaster all over the mould.

Make sure you make the plaster tile about 1.5cm deep as a minimum for a 20cm square mould. Give it a very gentle wiggle after all the plaster is in to level off the surface, and then leave it on a level surface undisturbed.

After about thirty minutes, feel the plaster. If it feels only slightly warm and your nail does not leave a deep impression, then it is stable enough to de-mould. Support the back fully as you tap or peel away your cake mould. Carefully place the drying plaster with the prints facing you onto a work surface.

Very carefully peel away the different printing matrices, taking it slowly so as to not rip away chunks of plaster.

As you remove more layers further in the plaster, be more gentle when you peel back. Lino can take away small chunks of plaster, but this can be avoided if you go around the edge of the plaster with a chisel. It all depends on the effect you are looking for.

Sometimes the use of a small chisel, etching needle or similar tool can help lift out the edge of submerged lino so you can then peel away the rest.

Once all the matrices have been removed, you can see a bold, sculptural relief print emerge. The lino translates beautifully in plaster, the strong dry-point lines are clean but some of the finer monoprints lost some mid-tones. In future impressions it would be worth leaving more ink on the monoprint areas.

carving tools and ink it up using oil-based inks, and take a hand printed impression from the surface. If you wish the plaster matrix to last for an edition, you can seal the surface of the plaster with a plaster sealing agent to prevent it getting dusty and crumbling off as you roll up with ink. The plaster dust in the oil-based ink can also be quite appealing and add a stony quality to the finished impression. It is best to let the oil-based ink dry on the plaster before carving away the next reduction layer and inking up. The plaster does not respond well to cleaning up with oil.

When the plaster is drying, you can scratch and sand and carve into the surface of the plaster using various tools.

Dead Fox, Mary Dalton. This is a five-colour reduction print carved into a 20 × 20cm plaster tile. The colours are slightly chalky as they mix with the plaster dust, and the edges feathered, adding a beautiful quality to the work.

DÉCOUPAGE

No need to panic: this technique does evolve from découpage, but we will be applying it with some added funk. The basic principles of découpage allow the artist to apply a patterned paper to an object's surface and then the resultant surface can be varnished to be protected. This can be a brilliant way to apply

Scratching into the plaster surface can be a beautiful, direct line against the printed textures.

A detail of the work shows the plaster caught at the edge of the reduction carving, giving the impression wonderful texture.

printed textural effects to any three-dimensional object. It works best when we print upon ultra-thin Japanese paper, down to as low as 9 gms. These lightweight papers are like a see-through skin, but they are incredibly strong and pick up printed detail very well. The thin nature of the paper allows you to paste the printed paper to all manner of objects, no matter how undulating their surface, because it will just mould to it, like a second skin. The weight and variety of paper is worth testing out before fully starting a project. Some methods of printmaking, such as relief, require a marginally thicker paper so that it does not tear when pulling away from the thick, sticky ink.

The application of this technique is the interesting topic. We can look at how we technically cover items, but the true point of interest is that this allows printmaking to become sculptural. Printed surfaces can be applied to any sculptural form, keeping true to the surface textures. This sculptural form can then be integrated into installation, be a stand-alone sculpture or can be integrated with mixed media works. Suddenly and simply, printmaking is beyond paper.

PROJECT

COVERING OBJECTS IN PRINT

This project will show you how to apply hand-printed paper to a basic object. The weight of the paper will have an effect on how easily it will fit to tightly curved or detailed areas. The lighter the weight of Japanese paper, the easier it will mould to fiddly shapes. However, the lighter the paper, the trickier it is to glue in position without getting into a sticky mess. It can take a little practice. Here, I am using a 13 gms paper which has had a print already printed upon the surface and left to dry. I am using an abstract wooden doll shape to demonstrate this simple process.

Materials

- Japanese paper, under 10 gms printed with pattern
- Rice paste glue or a bookbinder's pH neutral PVA and small soft brush
- Object
- Scissors

Sealing

The printed objects can be sealed with a varnish of your choice. This can protect the paper and also weatherproof it, depending on your varnish choice. Some oil-based varnishes will change the textural appearance of the paper, so it is worth having a test before committing.

TEXTILES

Printing upon the surface of textiles is nothing new. It has probably pre-dated the use of paper. The textiles tend to be used for items of clothing or homeware, but there is nothing saying that these printed surfaces cannot be used in sculptural forms. There are specific textile printing inks on the market, which allow you to more easily hand-print relief works. However, the traditional oil-based printing inks also do a great job and save you having to purchase more supplies. You can print both relief and intaglio methods onto textiles, as long as you follow a few basic prompts. Sometimes, depending on the weave and thread count of the fabric, an intaglio print can pick up more detail on cloth than on paper.

We will be using a strong, quick-drying glue for this project, such as a PVA.

The smooth and continuous surfaces can get coated in paper easily.

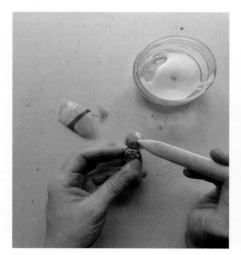
Using smaller sections of paper allows you to cover the detailed areas more easily.

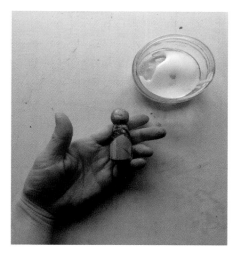

Once covered, leave the object for a few minutes to allow the glue to semi-dry.

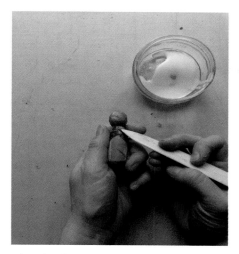

When the glue is almost dry, a bookbinder's bone or similar object can be used to smooth out any creases.

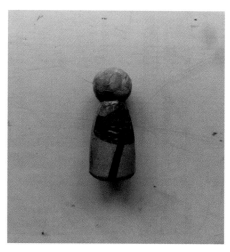

The completed little figure.

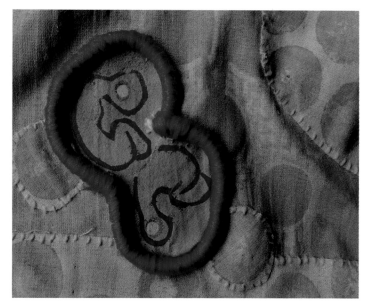

A detail of printed textile work using linocut and different stitches.

PROJECT

FABRIC PERSON

We will be looking at creating a fun fabric person using both hand printing and press printing. The project does not need to be followed along, it can just be witnessed and learnt from if you do not have access to all equipment. Furthermore, if sewing is not your strength, do not worry; this is to illustrate how textiles can give printmaking form and structure, so have a read and you can apply the techniques differently if you wish.

Materials

- Print workshop set-up
  We will be printing under a press and by hand, so a full set-up is required.
- Fabric
  You will need to source a high thread count (or tight, even weave) cotton, ideally neutral in colour. The weight should be that of a shirting cotton. You could use an old bed sheet or pillowcase. It will need to be ironed flat and cut into A4 sections (approximately).
- Selection of matrices
  We will be printing intaglio with paper dry-point, relief with lino and stamping and some monoprint under a press. Gather together options and then choose which you want to use as you read the project.
- Sewing facilities
  This is basic sewing, so can be done by hand or a simple machine.
- Stuffing
  We will be stuffing the figure to bring it to life. I will be using natural wool stuffing.

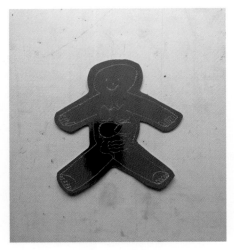

A piece of Tetra Pak cut to a figure and marks added to the surface.

The matrix inked up and wiped down, ready to print under a press.

Unbleached cotton fabric is dampened evenly using a water sprayer.

The damp fabric is placed on top of the inked matrix and printed.

The fabric is gently pulled from the matrix to reveal the print.

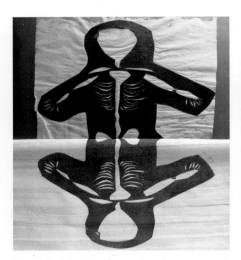

The back of the doll is created on a separate piece of fabric.

The front and back of the doll are left to dry completely.

The two are sewn together inside out and turned the right way. Leave a hole in the head to stuff the doll.

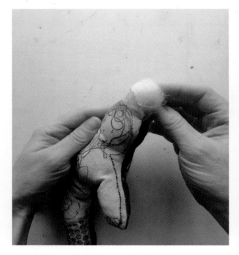

The doll is stuffed using 100 per cent wool stuffing.

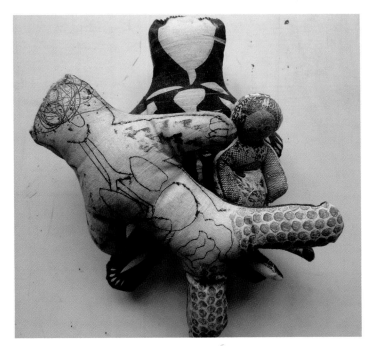
The hole in the head is sewn up and the doll is complete.

A completely dry print of approximately A4 in size is chosen.

OILED PAPER

Traditional paper umbrellas are made from oiled paper. They are naturally water repellent due to the paper being sealed with an oil that will resist the rain. This principle is very exciting for printed sculptural forms, as it offers the potential of outside display. Oiling paper is a brilliant way not only to add an element of water resistance but also to make it marginally transparent, offering a whole new perspective on paper. If using traditional oil-based printing ink, then applying a layer of oil all over the paper once the ink is dry will not affect the ink in the slightest. The oiling process also makes the paper stiffer, so it becomes perfect for sculptural construction.

PROJECT

OILED PRINTED PAPER LANTERN

This project perfectly illustrates how the oiling of paper changes its nature in relationship with printmaking. You will need to use linseed oil as this is a drying oil, which is essential if you do not want your lantern to remain oily.

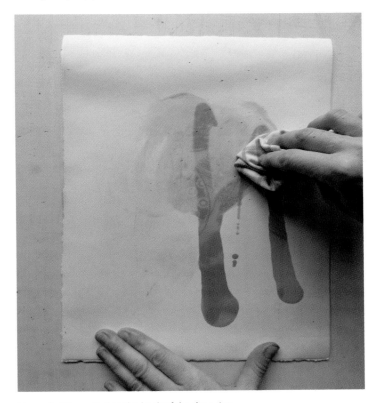
Linseed oil is applied to the back of the dry print.

Materials

- Linseed oil
- Old dry print

About A4 in size and (crucially) printed in oil-based inks and bone dry. The paper needs to be a minimum of 180 gms for this particular project.
- Clean cotton rag
- Needle and thread
- Small candle

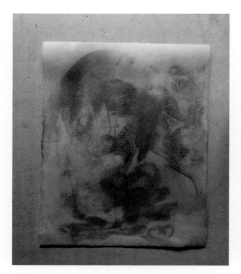

The linseed oil is spread out with a rag until covering the sheet.

The print is left to dry and then folded into a concertina.

The completed concertina is stiff and strong.

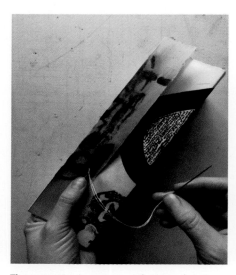

The concertina is sewn up at the two edges to form a folded tube.

The completed lantern shows the fold lines, giving it shape.

The lantern can be used to carefully cover a small candle. Never leave the lantern or candle unattended.

THINKING OUTSIDE THE BOX

Printmaking can be so flexible and applied to so many different substrates that it lends itself naturally to installation projects. It takes some planning of both technique and space to integrate traditional printmaking into installation, but the results are always fascinating. In my installation *Out of The Woods, Into The Trees*, I used traditional linocut techniques applied to both objects and fabric, as well as casting engraving textures into plaster forms. The techniques allowed me to apply the printed texture I wished upon the installation with both energy and control.

The artist Alexa Hatanaka works across disciplines, integrating printmaking into many of her pieces. She uses traditional processes and materials such as indigo dyeing, momigami, and sumi ink, which reflect her heritage and communicate powerfully her stories. These operate in conjunction with printed materials and collected papers to produce stunning sewn works and sculptural installations. These showcase that printmaking is fresh, it is alive, and it can operate within any media.

Into the Woods, Out of the Trees, Mary Dalton. This installation involved printmaking in several aspects. It had hand-printed textile hands from the wall. The wall had plaster cast wood engraving nodules attached to it and the cedar wood roundels had 'figures' emerging from them made from various printed elements. Two large unique prints hung from the back wall. Printmaking does not always have to exist on paper. (Photo: AB)

A detail of the plaster cast nodule and printed textile hands from the installation. (Photo: AB)

Journey To Valhalla, Mary Dalton. This tree sculpture has various paper dry-point textile limbs attached to the branches. Printmaking can seamlessly interact with other sculptural elements. (Photo: AB)

Hand-printed textiles have many applications, from clothes to furniture, or wrapping cloths, such as these.

Hazmat (Fake Flowers on Snow), Alexa Hatanaka. Sewn washi (Japanese paper): Haini kozo from Kakishi Seishi, miscellaneous washi from Japanese Paper Place, woodcut, linocut, sumi ink, oil-based ink, indigo dye, kakishibu dye, madder dye. A stunning example of a mixed-media printed and sewn momigami suit. The paper crumpling technique of momigami allows the artist to treat the washi paper more like fabric, allowing for the paper manipulation and sewing seen here.

Hazmat (Fake Flowers on Snow), Alexa Hatanaka. A wonderful detail of the hazmat suit showing the integration of printed papers in the work.

Koinobori (eat rice, play with cats), Alexa Hatanaka. Sewn washi (Japanese paper): Haini kozo from Kakishi Seishi, miscellaneous washi from Japanese Paper Place, woodcut, linocut, sumi ink, oil-based ink, indigo dye, kakishibu dye, collected paper rice bags. A large-scale installation incorporating printmaking which challenges both the traditional outlook upon print and its application within the fine art sector.

THE FUTURE OF PRINTING

What can printmaking offer the world? It offers a means of expression that is fluid and dynamic. It can be whatever you wish it to be. Its principles are deeply rooted in the ancient blood of humans that stems from the very beginnings of a desire of humanity to express and tell stories. If it is to survive then we need to not only continue the traditional methods, but bring these aesthetically and technically into a contemporary arena. The methods of traditional printmaking are traditional only in method; the aesthetics and outcomes can be shaken up completely. This book has given a little insight into the possibilities of engaging with printmaking in a more dynamic and unique way. How this is taken forward into your own language is entirely up to you and must be engaged with fully, challenged at every turn and followed through with energy and passion. Unique, dynamic prints tell a story of humans and of making that is direct and unhindered. Have fun constructing them, engage in learning about them, give your energy to them and they will tell your stories with equal energy and passion.

Animation Tests II, Nina Gross.

Animation Tests I, Nina Gross. These dry-points are part of a series that formed a stop frame animation of a falling figure, from top to the bottom of the print. The use of hand wiping to change the atmosphere is exquisite and the idea of animating a print is beautiful.

Animation Tests III, Nina Gross.

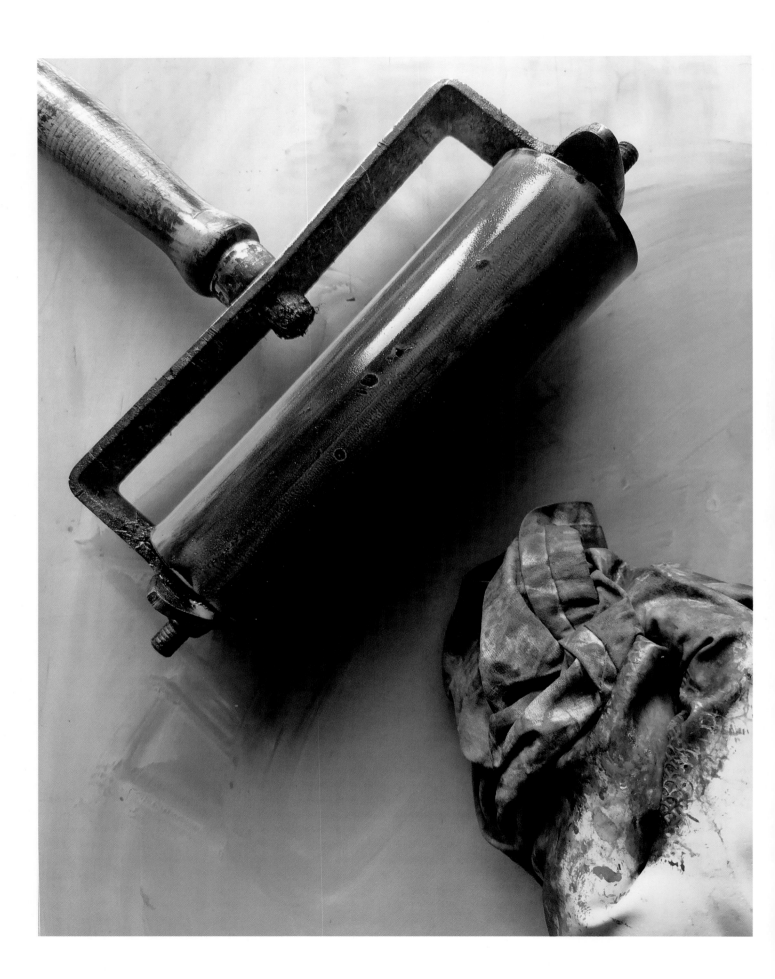

CHAPTER 10

WORKSHOP BASICS

n this chapter we will cover the workshop skills required for the processes in this book. Printmaking has such a range of technical set-ups and processes that we will only cover those required for the studies in this book. It should give you a good basic understanding of what is needed and a good stepping stone towards further investigation if you so wish. Some elements, such as registration, will only be broadly covered because the majority of work in this book focuses on unique, dynamic prints, of which registration for an edition or for certain elements is not the crucial component. Other techniques such as paper soaking will be covered in more depth, as this bears more relevance to many of the chapters. It is a chapter to be referred to when required whilst following the book's projects.

CREATING A PRINT SHOP ANYWHERE

Printmaking does not always need to happen in specialist studios. It can happen in the kitchen, in the woods, at festivals and fairs, and in homes and schools. Having the basic set-up to make your time printing more efficient, neat and enjoyable is about keeping it simple and organized. A good understanding of the processes you wish to explore can help influence how you should set up your space and manage the facilities required; once all of this is settled, you are more able to express freely. A printing press is required for some of the techniques in this book and you can purchase some wonderful tabletop etching presses that are neat, space efficient and produce great results. Whatever facilities are required, taking a bit of time organizing a workspace pays huge dividends in freeing up time to create.

Layout of Space

Working with oil-based ink can be a messy business. If possible, it is advisable to split your work area into the inky area, the clean area, and the printing area. In some cases where you have a smaller space and may be hand printing, the clean area also

A neat table set-up where inking is kept separate from hand printing.

translates as the hand printing area. Some of the hand printing techniques, such as stamping, will take inky materials across to your clean printing area, but by following a few of the basic practices of hand printing then the ink should really only remain on the matrix and not all over the work surface.

Many communal studios will have their own layout specific to use and the space. This is often laid out in a very logical manner and by working with it, your printing sessions will be a lot easier. If you have access to a press and print set-up at home, or in your personal studio, then designating an area for the inky work that is not near the clean paper or the press will help hugely. It is not always possible, and indeed in my own space, I have one worktop space (the top of a large plan chest) which is where I ink up. Due to the nature of the many colours and size of prints I work on, the whole space often becomes the inking area. To make sure that I have a space for clean paper and printing, the press I am using stays spotless, with no ink sitting on the press bed. The plan chest drawers are for the storage of clean blotters and paper, and if I am hand printing, I will do this on the clean extended press bed. Each space has its own difficulties and benefits. A small amount of time invested before starting to print to make the best of each space goes a long way to aiding a more fluid expression.

The Kitchen Table

More often than not, printmaking is done in the kitchen. I have done so myself, and still do, out of pure necessity of space. The same principles apply: designate a small section to the inky section, then a clean printing section, and – if using – a space to attach a pop-up table-top press. A huge amount can be achieved in small spaces. When working outside of a permanent set-up, it is always advisable to prepare items such as paper beforehand. It is really difficult and frustrating to cut down paper half-way through printing, when your hands are inky. If you have a nice stack of paper ready to go, then expression flows more freely. Sometimes when working in a small space it is advisable to work with one technique at a time, to fully engage and understand it. This way you can gather all required materials prior to commencing and you need not break the rhythm of making to disappear to get something.

It is not always possible to split spaces into inking areas and paper areas, as space will dictate otherwise. In these instances, the key is to remain neat and organized with a clear space for inking.

PAPER

The main substrate discussed in this book is paper. We have touched upon the use of textiles and other materials to receive a

A great example of a neat and clean print studio, with paper area on one side. The print room at West Dean College of Arts and Conservation, MFA department.

The Washroom Press, where Mary Dalton makes her work and research. Space has dictated the set-up, but it is still neat and organized.

printed impression, but the majority of work has been on paper. Paper is a wonderful substance and comes in many varieties, all of which have their own nuances.

Paper is categorized by weight, primarily in grams. Weight can vary hugely, from 9 gms to 300 gms. We have seen how different weights of paper respond to different techniques throughout the book. Printmaking paper is acid-free and generally has a pH of 7. The lack of acid in the paper means that it is archival, and the degradation of the paper is exceptionally slow. Newsprint has a high acidic content and will turn yellow readily in UV light. Paper is made across the globe and paper mills produce paper from cotton rag, mulberry bark, cellulose pulp, and many other materials. Many commercial papers are made by machine, but there are a few paper mills still making by hand, using the exceptional skill and knowledge of the paper makers to produce papers of the highest quality.

In Europe, pulp papers tend to be used. These papers are made from the pulp of a material, such as cotton rag. They will be what we have been primarily using in this book. Japanese washi paper is made differently, and contains long fibres of various plants and barks, such as mulberry bark, giving it a very strong and distinctive quality.

Soaking Non-Washi Papers

If using traditional European pulp paper to print with and it requires to be printed damp, then you can prepare it in advance of printing to make sure it is evenly soaked. This method is great if you have a set day on which you are printing and you have a batch of paper you are using. If you are printing more fluidly and impulsively, then there may not be time to pre-soak paper, which is why we talk about the surface dampening methods of

a sponge or a spray bottle. The pre-soaking of paper does make a difference to fine details in a dry-point or a monoprint, so is worth taking the time to prepare.

You will need access to a water bath, or a sink or bathtub that can fit your paper and hold about 2 inches of clean, cold water. You will also need two sheets of clean glass or Perspex sheet that fit your paper, plus about a 1-inch border all the way around. Finally, you will need some large blotting paper sheets. These are readily available from printmaking or paper stockists. The blotters can be dried out and re-used after each paper preparation. A good set will last years. If you have prepared a stack of damp paper and do not use it all, you need to let it dry out, otherwise the dampness in it will cause it to go mouldy. Just lay or hang the individual sheets up and then when ready to use, you can just give it a quick spray, since the paper has already been soaked.

Drying Prints

If you have been printing upon damp paper, then to prevent buckling of the wet paper as it dries, you need a method to allow it to dry flat. There are two main ways to approach this: under weights or stretched onto a board. If you dry prints under a weight then it will take longer for them to dry than if you stretch each individual print out upon a backing board. If you take the stretching route, each print requires its own backing board, which is not always available. If you dry under weight, you will need a space to allow the prints to sit under weight for a few weeks until dry. There are many advantages and disadvantages to each method, and it is best to choose the one appropriate to your working space, your facilities and how many prints you need to dry. If you have only got one print to dry, then stretching it on a board to let it dry overnight makes complete sense. If you

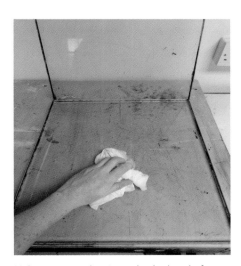
Make sure your glass is spotlessly clean before you commence.

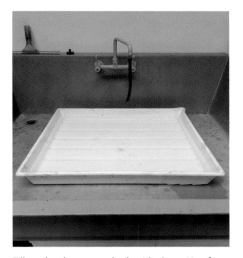
Fill up the clean water bath with about 3in of clean water.

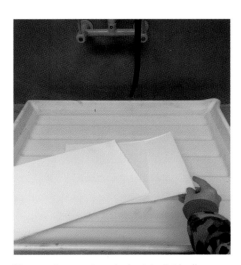
Place each paper into the bath individually, sliding one under the other.

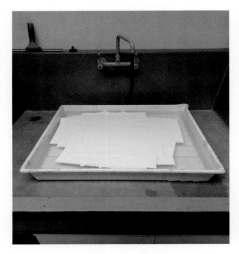

Once in, leave the paper for approximately twenty minutes to soak.

After twenty minutes, gently encourage all the paper together.

Lift up the paper and hold to drain until there is only a drip.

Place the whole damp paper block on the bottom clean glass.

Place the top glass down and weight if necessary. Leave overnight.

Take the paper out and place individual sheets between blotters. Pat down and re-stack the blotted paper under the glass sandwich. When ready to print, remove one sheet and replace the glass.

have created an edition of 30 prints, then drying them in a stack under weight would make more sense.

In order to dry under weight, you need to layer the damp prints between drying boards. These boards need to be made of a material that will adsorb the water from the paper and it will eventually evaporate through the exposed sides, thus drying the prints. You can buy professional printmaking compressed boards, but you could also use MDF boards or compressed grey card. It needs to be around 6mm thick as a minimum. You will also need a pile of clean, acid-free tissue paper and some heavy weights, such as bricks or weightlifting rounds. It can take up to two weeks for the prints to completely dry. After a week take a sample out from under the boards and leave

it for a minute. If it is still flat, then you know it is dry. If it is starting to buckle ever so slightly, then it is still damp and needs longer.

Stretching Paper

If choosing the stretching method, you will need to have access to a board larger than your impression paper and some traditional gum tape. The board needs to be clean, sturdy and level. Plywood, MDF or a similar material works well. The stretching method will mean you lose some of the border of your impression paper, so please do be aware of this when printing. The damp print will need to be placed in the middle of the board. Tear gum tape strips to the length of the four sides, plus a couple of inches

Place the damp print on top of clean tissue on the drying board.

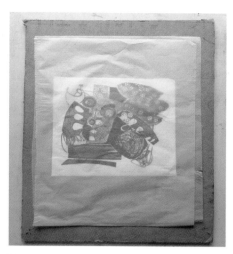
Place tissue on top. You may place prints next to one another.

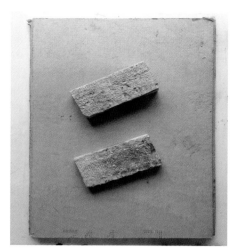
Place the board on top and weight. Leave until prints are dry.

Place another pre-dampened medium-weight paper over the top.

Place the washi paper onto some pre-dampened medium-weight paper.

excess. Using a wet sponge, run water over the gum side of the tape and stick this down halfway on the paper edge of one side, and halfway on the board. Repeat for the remaining three sides. The print will be dry overnight, so it is quick and effective.

Flattening Washi Papers

Light- to medium-weight washi papers require a slightly different treatment to flatten. They cannot be soaked so readily as a pulp-based paper and so to dampen and flatten we need to take a different approach. They need to be sandwiched between two previously soaked and blotted cartridge papers and then put between boards and placed under weight. The moisture from the pulp paper will soak into the Japanese paper and relax the fibres so that as it dries under the weight, it will dry flat. Therefore, you will require the same materials for drying under weight as before.

A print stretched with traditional gum tape and drying.

Paper fingers help grip paper without leaving inky finger marks.

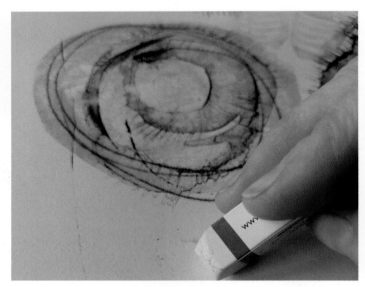

A clean white eraser can be used to help remove unwanted surface fingerprints.

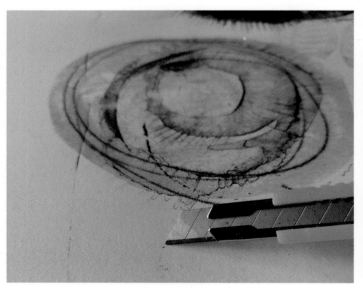

A sharp craft knife can flick off any unwanted tiny spots of ink.

Keeping Paper Clean

Keeping paper clean whilst printing is always easier said than done, particularly in the flow of expressive and dynamic print-making. It comes with practice and with the help of a few good tips that become like second nature the more you print.

The first is paper fingers. Paper fingers allow you to handle your paper even with inky fingers. The paper finger gets inky, and not the impression paper. They are brilliant and easily made from scrap medium-weight paper. You can also purchase or make thin metal ones if you wish.

Any light fingerprint marks on impression paper can be very gently removed once the ink is bone dry. Using a white eraser, you can very gently rub them out, which will marginally change the paper surface, but it does dissipate the visual appearance of the fingerprint. You can also use a scalpel to very gently flick off any very small specs or spatters of unwanted ink.

Tearing Paper

Tearing non-washi papers is reasonably straightforward and with a metal edge or ruler you can tear the paper well. This will give you a torn effect edge, similar to the deckle of the actual paper edge. You can also cut the papers with a sharp knife to give a crisp edge, which can be more useful for registration purposes.

If you have left no paper to tear, or the border is very tight, then there is a little makeshift method to create a rough edge. Place the paper with the edge overhanging a worktop by a

Tear the paper edge against a metal ruler or metal paper edge.

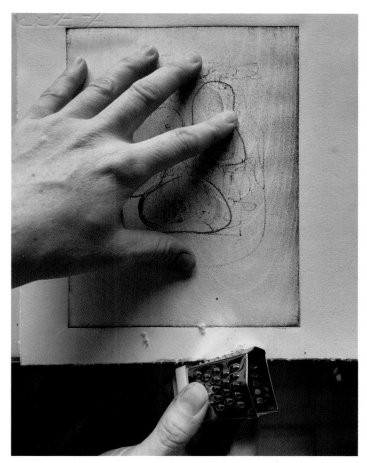

A grater can help lessen the harsh appearance of a cut edge if there is not enough paper available to tear.

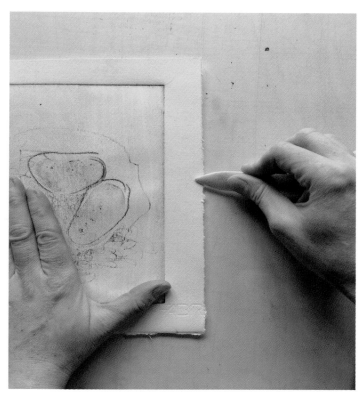

A paper bone can help flatten out the tear. You can press on the front or back of the paper, depending on the side you tore the paper against.

fraction of a millimetre and very gently grate the edge of the paper with a fine grater.

Tearing washi paper can be tricky, because of the long fibres in the actual paper. Try it. It is amazing how strong the paper is. One way will tear more easily than the other. If wishing to create a torn edge all around the print, you can cut the paper with a very sharp blade and then tease out the long fibres to generate a rough edge.

Hanging Up Prints

Having a suspended space to hang prints printed upon dry paper is a brilliant use of space. If you can create a pulley system to winch up a drying rack, then this is not only space efficient, but exceptionally useful. Drying racks can be made from basic materials such as a clothes peg attached to a bar, or they can be custom-made ball racks. Ball racks are worth every penny, as they allow you to put in and remove a print without having to touch the drying system with inky fingers. They also leave absolutely no emboss on papers, which pegs can sometimes do. Pegs and other devices involve you having to handle the peg, which can risk getting ink near a clean paper drying system. However, it is all space and budget dependent. There are many options available, so take a look and see which suits your set-up.

Clothes hangers can be a cheap and useful way to hang prints, although they can get inky and leave an emboss on the paper.

Ball racks are brilliant at hanging prints securely without any risk of an emboss.

Paper is slipped up into a ball rack slot. The marble is rolled up as the paper goes in. As the marble falls back down with gravity, it grips the paper tight.

A clean pole is used to push the marble back up to loosen the pressure. This allows you to retrieve prints without having to go near the drying system with inky fingers.

PRINTING PRESSES

Printing presses come in many varieties. They all have uses and application suited to one or many processes. Platen presses are ones that have a top and bottom flat surface, or platen, and the print gets sandwiched between the two platens as pressure is applied. These tend to work very well for relief work and occasionally collagraph or blind embossing. They do not print intaglio or lithographic work very well at all. You can get many designs of these presses, from the old cast-iron nipping presses, to floor standing varieties and modern, lightweight tabletop presses.

Etching presses come as geared presses or direct drive presses. Geared presses, by the nature of the gearing, are able to deliver a higher pressure output from the power applied by the artist. The direct drive presses are turned purely by the physical effort of the artist, the power input is equal to the pressure output. The handle is directly linked with the bottom roller, with no gearing in between. Thus they will never be able to reach the higher pressures of a geared press. The direct drive presses are significantly cheaper and a great starter option. You can get small tabletop varieties that due to the nature of the smaller width press beds will print at higher pressure than the larger varieties.

Geared etching presses are worth every single penny. They are heavy machines and the best quality ones tend to be cast iron, with large and heavy bottom rollers. Most communal studios will have one and you will notice the difference in quality of print with any intaglio method. The finer details and marginal variances in plate tone are picked up, giving the print more depth and life. Making a beautiful printing press is a huge skill and there are only a few companies left who make them from scratch. Never, ever, underestimate the worth of a high-quality press. If you do purchase one, they require looking after like any other piece of machinery. They will require oiling, greasing and cleaning. But this is part and parcel of a print studio and something that should be relished.

Setting the Etching Press Pressure

Setting up an etching press need not be daunting. Each press is different, and it is important to seek advice if you are at any point uncertain. Etching presses come with press blankets, which are traditionally made of high density felt. They help to distribute the pressure evenly across the printing plate and absorb excess water from damp paper if editioning. When printing intaglio it is common to use a set of three blankets: two facing blankets nearest the press bed and the swan skin, which is a fluffier blanket on top. I would advise a set of three blankets for paper dry-point.

Heavy roller or geared presses often have a press key which allows you to turn the pressure screws. In communal studios, it is critically important to ask before resetting the pressure of any etching press. They are often set specifically for etching, which will also be perfect for paper dry-point, and thus do not need to be touched. However, some studios with modern etching presses loosen the pressure at the end of the day, so the following instructions are given from loosening pressure to applying new pressure. Direct drive etching presses have a top roller that raises according to the pressure applied by the top screws and thus the resistance from the springs. You will be able to see the roller raise or lower visually. In this instance, you can loosen and raise the top roller to slide your blanket set in. The pressure can then be set from the middle of the press bed. If you are printing a paper dry-point, I would advise putting a sample of the paper dry-point under the press and tighten to finger tight and then half a turn more. It will need heavy pressure to pick up the details. Lino will need less pressure. Pressure tests on the direct drive presses are always useful because their rollers are

A nipping press, or bookbinding press, is a great option for relief work.

A direct drive press can be a useful etching press starter option.

A beautiful example of a floor-standing cast-iron geared etching press.

always being moved up and down, so it is useful to know what pressure works well for what you are printing.

On heavy rolling presses, such as a Rochat, there is a system to follow to allow you to set the pressure. If blankets are in the press, you will need to loosen the top screws, roll the press bed to one end and roll out the blankets. You can now start over.

Harry Rochat is a press-making company based in the UK which makes presses of the highest standard.

Loosening the screws on a heavy rolling press to remove the blankets before setting a new pressure.

Firstly, roll the press bed to the middle of its length and tighten the pressure screws to finger tight. Make sure you turn each side evenly to make sure you are applying an equal pressure across the roller and bed. Once both are tight, you can add a small mark in the same position on each top screw to allow you to turn them the same amount in the future, knowing the pressure is even across the bed. Some presses have gauges, but others do not. The pressure from each screw needs to now be released enough to insert the blankets. It is generally advised to loosen each screw by three complete turns.

Next, roll the press bed to one end and lay out your blankets flat and evenly on the press bed. It can help if the blankets are slightly staggered at the edge that is closest to the roller to help the roller feed them in. Turn the press handle to feed the blankets in.

If wishing to print a thin paper dry-point, I would advise a marginally tighter pressure than this basic setting. Run the press to the middle of the press bed and add a half turn to each screw. This should suffice.

Once the basic pressure is set, it is highly advisable to test the pressure on some sample matrices. If it is printing well, you can note how many turns were added from the base pressure to achieve a good impression.

Take your time to know your press, be safe and if at any point you are having to force the press to turn, stop. The pressure is too

When ready, blankets are laid flat and staggered at the feeding end.

If printing a thin paper dry-point, you will need to increase the pressure marginally. This can be done when blankets are in and from the middle of the press bed.

Run the press bed to one end, ready to print.

high for your printing plate. Re-set and start again. It is common to have to tweak pressure when testing a print, but once a good pressure has been found, then it is best to leave it be.

Raising the Rollers

If you are printing a material of 1.5mm or more, it would be advisable to add runners on the press bed. The runners are the same depth as the matrix you are printing and help raise the rollers so that the press is not damaged or the work jolted as the rollers try to feed in the deeper matrix. Not all presses should have their rollers raised, particularly the older, heavy geared etching presses. It is worth finding out about your make or asking the studio before adding runners. Direct drive presses are fine to have their rollers raised as long as they can accommodate the depth.

The runners are ideally the length of the press bed and mostly made out of the same material as your matrix. If you are printing lino, the runners tend to be lino; if printing 4mm ply, the runners are a similar timber. This ensures the runners are the exact depth of the matrix. To insert the runners, you will need to loosen the press and set the pressure according to their depth. This requires you to loosen the screws completely and feed the runners under the roller when no blankets are in. You can slightly taper the edge of the runners to allow the roller to feed them in more easily. Then roll the press bed to the middle and follow the pressure setting as before. Once set, you are ready to print. Always note the end of the runners so that you do not run the roller off the end of the runners, which could cause it to clunk dramatically.

Correct depth runners are added under the blankets to set the pressure.

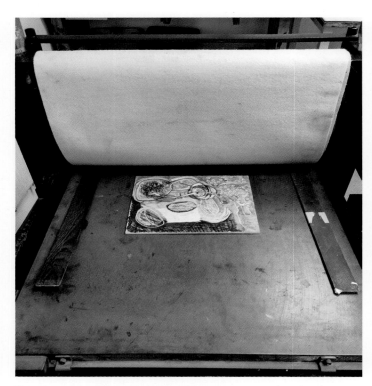
The print matrix of the same depth as the runners can now be printed.

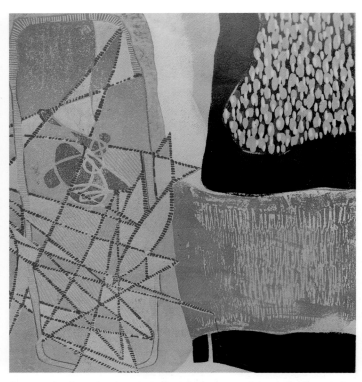
An example of good registration where the layers are sitting in the intended relationship with one another.

REGISTRATION

You will have noticed that in the 'Outside Drawing' project in Chapter 6, I used a quick registration method by using my eye to line up the piece of lino for sequential prints. Registration is talked about much in printmaking, and basically describes aligning more than one layer of printed marks according to the artist's wishes. This may be directly on top of the previous marks – thus registration needs to be in line with the previous layer – or it may be making sure that the relationship between areas of printed marks are the same across an edition, even if not on top of one another. Registration is also a way to ensure your printed area is sitting in the correct position in relationship to the paper area.

Registration methods vary greatly, and each artist will have a preferred method. Unless I am producing an edition, I will register by eye. I find it less hassle and less restrictive then setting up a formal registration system. Furthermore, I am training my eye and hand to register without the dependency upon any other system or materials. We will look briefly at a few of the most common methods of registration. If you are producing an edition of your work which requires a registration system, then stick to one method for the full edition. Changing halfway through can cause problems.

Template for Square-Edged Prints
Making or drawing out a template can help you register quickly and easily. You can draw out your template onto paper, a plastic sheet, or even directly onto the press bed. Some press beds even have grids added to aid registration. The key information needed on the template is the position of the matrix and the position of the paper. If drawing onto paper or plastic, when this template is positioned onto the press bed, place a piece of tissue paper over it before placing your matrix in position. You should be able to read the template through the tissue and it prevents ink transferring from the back of your matrix onto your template. If using plastic or the press bed to mark up, you can use a chinagraph pencil which can then be rubbed off after use. If printing with damp paper, marking plastic or the press bed is advisable because a paper template will eventually absorb moisture from the damp paper and buckle. Communal studios may have presses with grids drawn on the press bed which you can use, but rarely allow marking on the press bed, so please use another method in this instance.

The template method works well for more organic matrices or multiple matrices being printed at once.

Registration Boards
Registration boards are mainly used for hand printing and allow you to position paper and matrix in the exact relationship each time. It can at a push work for organic shaped matrices, but works best if you have straight edges. They can be made simply from grey board or card. Make sure the board you use is a lower depth then the matrix you are printing with.

Place the matrix on the registration template and draw around.

Mark the top of the matrix in relation to the top of the outline.

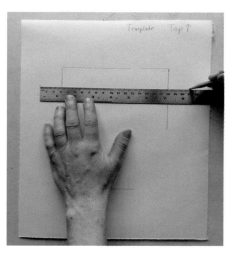

Measure out and draw the position of the paper in relation to the matrix.

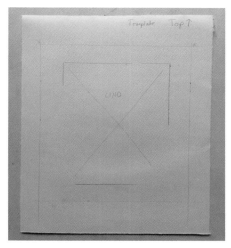

The completed simple, quick and effective registration template.

Place the organic matrix in position on the registration template.

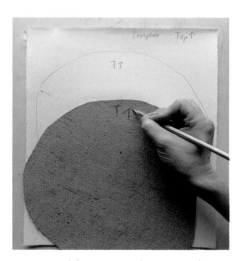

Draw around the matrix; mark a point on the matrix and a corresponding one on the template.

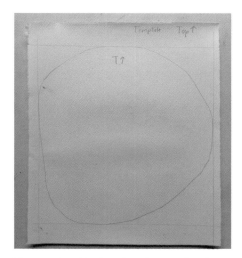

The completed basic registration template for a non-square matrix.

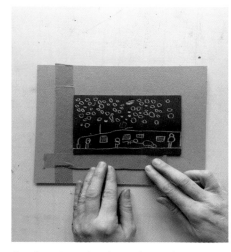

On a firm piece of card, wood or similar, tape down strips of thin grey board. These will keep the lino in its position.

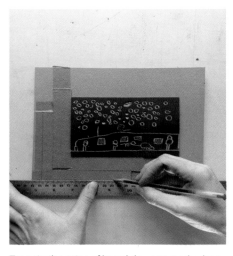

Tape similar strips of board down to mark where the edge of the paper will sit.

The paper can be placed in position using the guides on top of the inked-up lino.

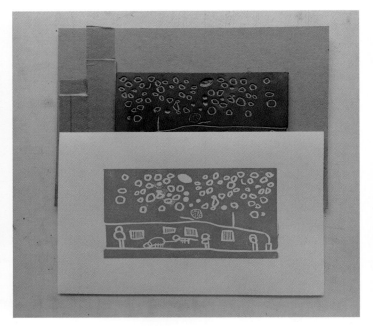

The completed impression printed in the correct position on the piece of paper. This method may be used for multi-plate or reduction work, making sure each time the lino and the paper sit against the board guides.

Ternes Burton Pins

These are especially designed for registering prints. They allow you to pin your paper in the exact place each time. They attach to the paper and pin into a corresponding tab on a registration board. You still need to find a way to place your matrix in position each time and each sheet of paper will need a pin.

Positioning of Parts

There will come a point when you want to position an element in an exact part of your impression, yet you are printing with the paper on top, so how can you see where it goes? You need to make a quick registration guide, which will help and allow you to position the elements. I will be using tissue paper to create this guide and transfer my reference points onto a backing piece of paper for my registration template. You may also use a thin sheet of acetate to trace over your key parts of your print and your paper, and use this directly as

Use the tissue and a pencil to trace your key elements of the print and the position of the paper.

Flip the tracing paper over and place on top of a medium-weight paper. Draw over your pencil marks with another pencil, thus transferring them onto the thicker paper.

Place any matrix or elements in their position on the paper registration sheet.

Bunt Line, A.M.R. Street. Hand-printed cards are a popular item to edition.

your registration guide. I am trying to avoid the use of the plastic and the method described here works well for unique prints. If you are editioning and you are using damp paper, then a plastic-based guide would work better as it would not get damp.

EDITIONING

Creating an edition of a print using the techniques we have explored can be tricky. In fact, the very nature of this book is to encourage unique prints, but as we have mentioned, editioning has its place in printmaking and so we will look at it briefly. The techniques we are exploring are designed to celebrate the unique print, created purely for that one moment of expression. If you still wish to create an edition, then lino is easily re-printable, as is a shellac sealed card matrix. If you are wishing to edition a reduction lino, then you will need to print the edition as you cut each layer, since you cannot go back to the previous layer. Thus, if you wish for ten prints in red, you print the ten, then you cut and ink up the blue and print the blue over your red.

The stamping methods are free-form, so if you wish to reproduce them it would be technically described as a varied edition. This means you are attempting to recreate the same image to the best of your abilities, but some of the techniques make this technically impossible, thus it is a varied edition. You would need to judge with your eye where the stamps go, perhaps following a drawn registration guide as a demarcation of area.

CLEANING UP

Cleaning up oil-based ink is really easy. You do not require any solvent of any description, only vegetable oil and cotton rags. Many of the ecological clean-up solvents on the market are not as sustainable as they are marketed to be and I still stay well clear of them. Vegetable oil is inert to humans and the planet. If you wish to keep your footprint on the earth even lighter, many places now stock locally sourced oils at a very good cost, which reduces miles travelled.

Using gloves for clean-up is optional. Any ink left on your hands will come off using a small dab of vegetable oil and then soap, and any staining eventually washes off. You can get plant-based plastic washing up gloves now and these provide excellent protection when it gets very inky during clean-up.

SUSTAINABLE APPROACHES

It is so important that we are aware of how we can change day-to-day practices to lessen our footprint upon the earth. Small steps in the studio do not need to hinder expression and if all artists are to take such an approach, then it will benefit all, for now and the future.

One of the biggest print shop switches is to use oil instead of solvents for clean-up. In conjunction with old cotton sheeting

Pour about a 50p sized amount of oil on the inking surface.

Using the roller, roll the oil out over all inky surfaces.

With a dirty rag, wipe away the first layer of black ink.

Wipe away the ink from the roll-up surface.

Wipe the ink off the roller, including the edges.

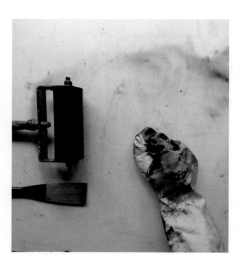

Move onto a clean rag to remove the last of the ink.

Give the roller a final wipe, including the edges.

Using a diluted soap solution, pour some on the inking surface.

Wipe down the last grease from the surface with a washable cloth.

as rags, or similar, then you are really making ground in a more sustainable practice. If you are using a degreaser to remove the last residue of oil from any surfaces, you can make your own with vinegar or lemon juice, or even by dissolving some simple bar soap in warm water. Both of these can be added to a re-usable spray bottle and used in conjunction with a washable cleaning up cloth to remove that last oily residue.

Many printmaking sundries can be re-used before they get binned. Newsprint and tissue paper that has been used for protecting the press bed or similar can be re-used, even with ink on it. Once the ink has dried, the papers can be used again and again.

Cleaning up rags can also be used many times before finally binning or recycling them. If you have a rag with a lot of ink and oil on, just hang it up to dry for a few days, and it can be re-used to remove the worst of the ink of the next clean-up. Rags that are half dirty can be re-used the next time, and so on. You will be surprised how many times they can be re-used before finally having to recycle them.

Replacing masking tape with biodegradable gum tape or the pre-gummed masking tape is a great switch: simple and effective.

Some of the processes in this book use water, such as the lithographic methods. If available, I will always use rainwater instead of tap water. Water is a valuable and important resource and if we can use an alternative to drinking and cooking water, then all the better.

Rags can be reused to an extent before binning.

Newsprint and tissue paper can be reused when the ink has dried.

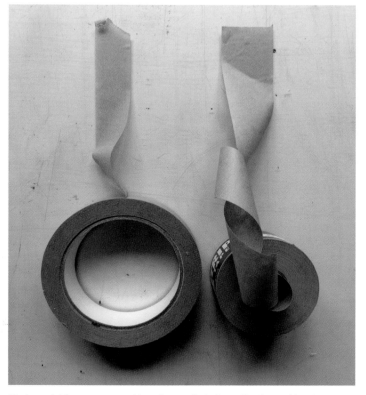

Biodegradable pre-gummed tape is a perfect alternative to masking tape.

Re-using printing matrices is a common occurrence throughout the book. They offer new textures and approaches to making an impression and some, such as lino, can be re-used in multiple different techniques before they eventually start to wear out. It is always worth keeping a box of lino off-cuts around to have a rummage for pattern or textures.

MAKING DRY-POINT CARD

The dry-point card we have been using in this book up to now has been based upon a plastic-coated thin card. This could have been re-used from a carton or bought in new – both of which still involve the use of a thin plastic coating glued upon an otherwise recyclable product. Some of the drinks cartons are now being made out of plant-based plastic, which is a huge step in the right direction. However, I have come up with an alternative to the plastic coating, which allows you to create very similar marks and prints. Of course, it is not exactly the same, but all the principles explored in the dry-point chapter relate to this home-made version, the end print may be marginally different. You will need grey board 1mm or 2mm thick and some natural hard wax oil.

Cut your grey board to size and coat with an even layer of hard wax oil.

After each layer is dry, apply another layer. Three layers works well.

When completely dry, you can treat the board as you would Tetra Pak.

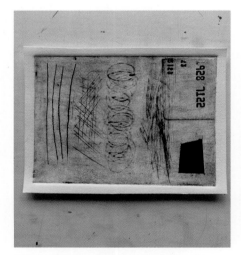

Ink up as for paper dry-point and print onto damp paper under a press.

Picking Purslane, Mary Dalton. This print was made on a sheet of home-made paper dry-point and treated as a roll-over, rather than an intaglio.

STOCKISTS AND RESOURCES

Intaglio Printmaker
www.intaglioprintmaker.com
@intaglioprintmaker
General print supplies, palette knives, inks, books, consumables, paper, dry-point card, and all printmaking supplies related to lithography.

Hawthorn Printmaker Supplies
www.hawthornprintmaker.com
@hawthorn_printmaker
Specialist print supplier. I use them a lot for high-quality rollers and inks/pigment.

Hand Printed
www.handprinted.co.uk
@handprinteduk
A great general printmaking supply store. They also run classes and have regular online blog updates and demonstrations.

Jackson's Art Supplies
www.jacksonsart.com
Good range of print supplies, especially for the lower budget with quality still intact.

Cranfield Colours
www.cranfield-colours.co.uk
@cranfieldcolours
Suppliers of traditional printmaking inks. Wonderful quality and range.

Essdee
www.essdee.co.uk
@essdee_uk
Suppliers of traditional lino in packs and large rolls. Also stockists of other lino supplies.

John Purcell Paper
www.johnpurcell.net
@johnpurcellpaper
Basic website to give an overview of papers available. They are quick to respond via phone or email. They are a professional paper merchant, so better to order if getting a large amount of paper.

Shepherds London
www.store.bookbinding.co.uk
@shepherdslondon
A great paper supplier, covering a range of European and Asian papers. They also supply wonderful *chine-collé* and decorative papers.

Awagami Factory
www.awagami.com
@awagami_factory
The foremost washi paper making centre in Japan. They stock a full range of washi papers in a range of weights. All handmade using traditional methods.

Two Rivers Paper
www.tworiverspaper.com
@tworiverspaper
This wonderful paper-making mill still makes cotton rag pulp paper by hand. Stunning paper.

Harry F Rochat Ltd
www.harryrochat.com
@rochat_printing_presses
Makers and suppliers of some of the finest printing presses available.

The Washroom Press
www.pop-up-press.co.uk
@m_dalton_print
The home of Mary Dalton's outreach printing, it also has links to the YouTube channel which has many free 'how-to' printmaking videos.

Pfeil Tools
www.pfeiltools.com
For beautiful relief tools (and carpentry and other amazing tools).

The Plastic People
www.theplasticpeople.co.uk
For plastic cut to size for use in monoprints and roll-up surfaces.

INDEX

acetone 99
à la poupée 79–81
animation 185

ball rack 193–4
barren 24, 27, 37–38, 53
blankets 195–197
blend 157–159

carving (tools) 23, 24
   (process) 24, 26–27, 124, 129–131, 177
chine-collé 133, 134–138, 142, 146,
   168–170, 172
Chiyogami 134
cleaning 18, 201–203
CMYK 150
collage 54, 133–147
collage paper 142–144
collagraph 35–36
coloured pencil 165
colour test 31
colour lithography 127, 128–131
colour matching 31, 156–157
copper plate oil 11, 51, 150
cork 14, 35
corrugated card 14, 16–17
Cotgreave, Liz 168
Cranfield Colours 10
crayon (lithographic) 92, 93–94, 108,
   113, 121
   (wax) 163, 164–165
   (water soluble) 45, 50, 53
Creenaune, Danielle 103, 109

découpage 177–179
deckle 192–193
distilled water 101, 102
Donovan, Tara 9, 41
dremel 27, 30

Editioning 9, 23, 104, 201
emboss 58–59, 73–74, 105, 110
end grain 90
etching (lithography) 90, 95–96, 100,
   119, 127
etching needle 28–29, 69, 73, 176
etching press 44, 47, 54, 67, 89, 116,
   137, 187, 195–198
extender 149–154

first impression 15, 61, 78
Fenton, Anna 68
French chalk 92, 95, 113
fretsaw 107

ghost impression 15, 71, 78–79,
   164, 170
grater 22, 26, 28–29, 54, 65, 193
Gross, Nina 80, 185
gum Arabic 89, 92, 95–6, 119, 126
Gunning, Jemma 43, 44, 49

hand colouring 163–164
Hatanaka, Alexa 182, 184
handprinting 21, 27–28, 33, 53, 97–98,
   131, 187–188, 198
heavy roller press 195–198
hybrid 38–40, 85–86, 145–146,
   167–172

inking (lino) 26–29, 32–33, 35–36
   (lithography) 96–97, 109, 112, 113,
   120, 124, 129–131
   (technique) 56–57
   (intaglio) 69–71
ink transfer 98, 105, 111
installation 182–184
intaglio 65–66, 74, 83–84, 135, 139,
   163, 168, 178, 195, 204

Japanese vinyl 22
Japanese paper 28, 59, 91, 97, 121, 133,
   134, 139, 140–1, 146, 178, 184, 191

kitchen table 188
Kozo 133, 139

lino 21–36
lino tools 22, 27
lithino 115–131, 168–170
lithographic ink 118
lithography 6, 89–113, 115–131
linseed oil 10–11, 20, 82, 144–145,
   160–162, 181–182

mask 12–13, 15, 32–33, 39–40, 57–58,
   78–79, 87, 111–112, 126
matrix 9
mokulito 89–113
monochrome 43–63, 110, 126–127,
   160, 169
monoprint 6, 43–44, 49, 76–77, 80, 87,
   103, 127, 137–8, 164
multi plate 35, 85–86

netting 15
nipping press 195

oiled paper 144–145
opaque white 130, 153–154,
   162–163, 171

paper (cleaning) 192
   (deckle) 193
   (drying) 189–191
   (soaking) 189–190
   (stretching) 190, 192
paper dry-point 65–87, 204
pattern 13, 32, 35, 38, 133–44

pigment 10–11, 154

plaster 41, 173–177

plate grain 103, 116, 122

plaster (cast) 41, 173–177
    (print) 177

plywood 90–91, 93

portrait 45–48

primaries 150

printing dolly 11–13, 17–19

rag wiping 46, 49–50, 62

rain water 7, 92, 174, 203

reduction 30, 34, 116, 129–131, 171,
    174–177

registration 32, 34, 192, 198–201

reticulation 101–102

rice paste glue 134, 139

Rochat 196, 205

roller effects 157–160

roll over 54, 81–82, 161

rubbing tablet 92, 94

runners 197–198

sculpture 173

scumming up 113

side grain 90

single pull 43–63

softcut 22

stick tusche 92–94, 102

stone lithography 115

Street, A.M.R. 201

Street, Guiwenneth 66

table top press 67, 195

talc 92, 100, 119

tape 163, 190, 203

Ternes Burton pins 200

textiles 73, 178–181

Tetra Pak 45, 54–56, 60, 66–67, 85, 103,
    180, 204

tramlines 113

true grain 52–53

Tusche 92–94, 102, 125–126

varnish 35, 100–101, 177–178

viscosity 50–51

viscosity printing 160–162

wallpaper rollers 35–36

washi 189

Washroom Press 188, 205

watercolour 53, 109–110, 112,
    163–164

West Dean College of Arts and
    Conservation 188

wiping down 70, 76, 79–80,

woodcut 91, 104–106, 112, 184

workspace 11, 187–188

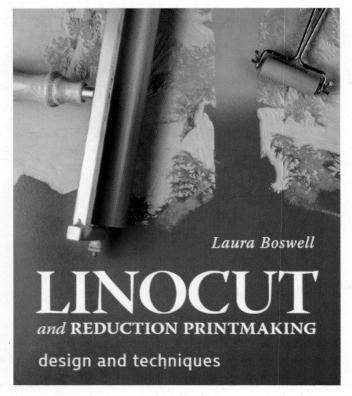

Laura Boswell

LINOCUT
and **REDUCTION PRINTMAKING**

design and techniques

978 0 71984 031 9

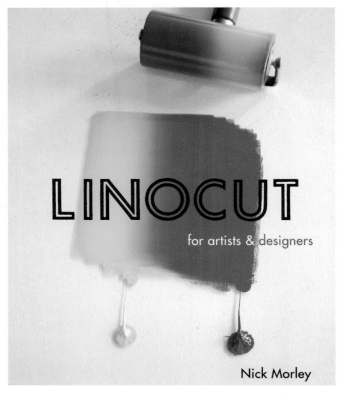

LINOCUT

for artists & designers

Nick Morley

978 1 78500 145 1

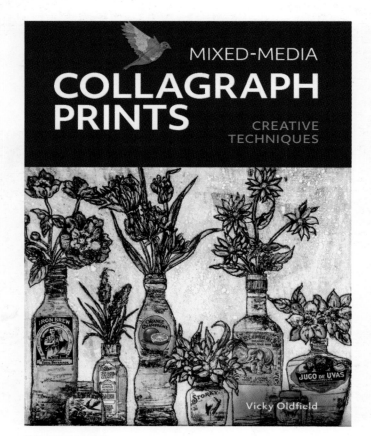

MIXED-MEDIA
COLLAGRAPH PRINTS

CREATIVE TECHNIQUES

Vicky Oldfield

978 0 71984 106 4

SCREENPRINTING ON TEXTILES
The Complete Guide

Sue Westergaard

978 1 78500 753 8